PARABLES *and*
Passion

PARABLES *and*

JESUS' STORIES
FOR THE
DAYS OF LENT

JOHN INDERMARK

UPPER
ROOM BOOKS®
NASHVILLE

Cover design: Bruce Gore/Gore Studio
Cover art: Steven D. Purcell
Second printing: 2007

Library of Congress Cataloging-in-Publication

Indermark, John, 1950–
    Parables and Passion: Jesus' stories for the days of Lent / John Indermark.
        p. cm.
    ISBN 13-digit: 978-0-8358-1005-X
    ISBN 10-digit: 0-8358-1005-4
    1. Lent—Meditations.   2. Holy Week—Meditations.   3. Jesus Christ—Parables—Meditations.   I. Title.
    BV85.I45 2006
    242'.34—dc22   2006008617

Printed in the United States of America

To

Isabel Riepenhausen

Whose ears are just now beginning to hear the stories

that reveal who she is and who she may yet be

as a beloved child of God

CONTENTS

ACKNOWLEDGMENTS

I remember the storytellers in my life: my grandmother, who would read to me; my Sunday school teachers at Salvator Evangelical and Reformed Church, who emphasized the stories told in scripture. I remember listening on several occasions to Fred Craddock, Emeritus Professor of Preaching and New Testament at Candler School of Theology, who reminded many of us that the gospel is sometimes best encountered in the story of another overheard as if it were our own—because it is.

I am grateful to the folks at Upper Room Books who have given me the privilege for some years now to voice my stories in the printed word. And let me be quick to point out, they have not been content to let me say just any old (or new) word as I please without regard to how it sounds or what sense it makes or not. Editors like JoAnn Miller, Rita Collett, and Jeannie Crawford-Lee have done their level best to make me a better writer and my books a better read. I am grateful to them for their caretaking, in the best sense of that word, with my words. Denise Duke and Sarah Schaller-Linn have attended to matters of verification and copyright. And I am also grateful to Sarah for all that she does behind the scenes to strive for publication of such works in tongues other than English.

Other writers I encounter along the way continue to nurture my writing. On an ongoing basis I get to listen to the stories of Jenelle Varila and Brian Harrison in the triad that forms our monthly writing group. This past year, Amy Jauch Woodward at Mo-Ranch in Texas gave me the opportunity to colead a writer's workshop with Jan Epton Seale, a gifted poet from the lower Rio Grande Valley. A special thanks to Sharon Harding from the

Seasons of the Spirit community (see below) whose comments as a reader brought sharper focus to this work.

I need to say a special word about another community of writers I have on several occasions now had the privilege to join. *Seasons of the Spirit* is a lectionary curriculum both ecumenical and international in scope. The meetings of writers and editors are a weeklong immersion in scripture and community. The weeks I have shared with these people have been transformative, not just for my writing but for my Christian experience. They have helped shape the lines of this book in deep ways.

Finally, ten years ago I wrote in the acknowledgments of my first book: "I owe thanks and far more to Judy and Jeff Indermark for allowing husband and father the gift of spending inordinate amounts of time before a computer screen in order to cultivate a ministry of the written word." As much as things change, some things stay the same. My gratitude to family for support and love and encouragement go beyond my ability to frame words, especially today. I write this fourteen hours after Judy and I got a late-night phone call from Jeff, who had been in an accident. He was fine, his car absolutely totaled. So I offer this closing acknowledgment of gratitude with a bit more edge than I might have yesterday. And I do so with the reminder that it is well and good to speak and write such words in the times we are given to the ones we are given by the grace of God.

BEFORE YOU BEGIN
A Word about Parables

*W*hat is a parable? Exact definitions vary from "stories of life with religious or spiritual lessons" to "metaphors or similes that take narrative form." The opening chapters of some books on Jesus' parables deal extensively with issues of definition, interpretation, and background. If you have interest in a more academic companion to read alongside this work, I would commend two books. *The Parables of Jesus: A Commentary* by Arland J. Hultgren and *Hear Then the Parable: A Commentary on the Parables of Jesus* by Bernard B. Scott provide helpful insights into the background of parables.

What has been *my* operating understanding of parable in this book? Some readings on Celtic spirituality have impressed me with the idea of "thin" places. As I understand the concept, these are locations with some tradition of religious or spiritual meaning attached to them. "Thin" refers to a mystical way in which the usual boundaries between heaven and earth, sacred and secular, holy and ordinary seem to melt away in such places: Iona, Lourdes. You might name places of importance peculiar to your spiritual journey and experience. For me the parables are thin places in Jesus' teachings. By showing us ordinary elements and experiences, parables provide a transparency to see the whole of our lives—and the holy in our lives—in a new way.

We cannot truly say that Jesus invented the parable; Hebrew Scriptures have precedents for this form of teaching (for example, Isaiah 5:1-7 or 2 Samuel 12:1-4). Nor would it be true to suggest that parables are unique to Jesus. Some ancient Jewish sources compile parables taught by other rabbis of Jesus' era and the decades following. But it would be true to affirm that the church knows parables primarily through the teachings of Jesus. This form is the most distinctive of Jesus' teachings, and this book explores them in the context of the distinctive season we call Lent.

Why use parables to explore Jesus' passion? This book does not intend to argue that the parables are *really* about that final movement in Jesus' journey toward and in Jerusalem summarized in the word *passion*. However, as Lent in general and Holy Week in particular do bring to a head the nature of God's reign revealed by the Messiah (Christ) of God, parables and passion fit together. We read the parables through the lenses provided by Jesus' passion. We gain insight into the meaning of that passion through these "thin" stories where common and Holy touch each other and draw us in to their convergence.

A further word is in order about God's kingdom or realm. Many of the parables identify their intent as revealing some aspect of God's sovereign realm (kingdom of God or heaven). Some people may hear that as saying these parables reveal what life will be like in the afterlife. Certainly God's reign points toward the future. Clearly, the qualities of that realm have not been fully realized on earth. We wait and hope with longing for such fulfillment. *But* the reign and realm of God begins now, in our midst. "The kingdom of God is among you" (Luke 17:21), Jesus said. The parables are not about pie-in-the-sky theology; they describe the qualities and characteristics of God's reign that intend to transform how we live on *this side* of the grave. We need not wait until after death to live in God's presence. That gift and calling is ours now. The parables invite us to consider that truth by using common images and experiences of life now to reveal God's reign. Lent offers a season in which to reflect on that truth as we witness how Jesus lived in the presence of God on the journey that leads to Jerusalem, an upper room, a killing hill, and an emptied tomb.

Using the Book

Parables and Passion is intended to be read over a six-week period in the season of Lent, one chapter per week. Each chapter has five daily readings and an introductory overview to the week's theme. Consider reading the overview the first day of the week, the five readings on each of the next five days, and then observe a weekly sabbath from reading. You might spend that last day revisiting the overview and reflecting on what you read. Those who participate in a group study may use the sabbath as the group meeting day.

Each daily reading consists of a text reference to a parable, the reading that grows out of that parable, a prayer, and a spiritual exercise. Please read the parable first. It sets the stage for the reflective piece to follow. And do not neglect to do the daily spiritual exercises, which connect each day's theme with your own spiritual journey and growth.

Find a time of day when you can do the daily readings with adequate opportunity to focus upon these words and their speaking to you. Unless there are extenuating reasons, do not try to cram a whole chapter into one day. Be patient. Let each day's reading be sufficient for that day. Allow the content and reflection to build over the course of days.

I have included a prologue for Ash Wednesday and an epilogue that contains readings for the concluding days of Holy Week: Maundy Thursday, Good Friday, Holy Saturday, and Easter Sunday. As a result, the book can become a daily Lenten companion beginning Ash Wednesday and concluding Easter Sunday, with the exception of the weekly sabbaths for reflection. You may need to adjust how and when you do your daily readings if you are part of a study group, depending on your meeting day.

If you have a leadership role in a group study of this book (or are just curious), the session guides at the end of the book are prefaced by instructions for their use.

ASH WEDNESDAY

I once helped facilitate a retreat for a neighboring congregation. Among the participants was a young man in his late twenties or early thirties. He was new to the church—not simply to this congregation but to Christian community as a whole. He did not possess the religious vocabulary or ingrained set of images of someone raised in the church. During one group discussion he kept raising questions about some basic elements of Christian theology. The group members' answers did not seem helpful. I began to realize that he lacked connection with our language and images.

What broke the impasse? The young man alluded to the way his studies in philosophy at college had strongly influenced his view of life, though he wondered how they fit in his newfound faith. I found myself answering him with language and concepts that stretched my memory back to courses in philosophy at university and in systematic theology at seminary. I don't know how others in that room received what I said but amazingly and graciously he understood. My words spoke to him and connected to his experience; he heard.

Hopefully, you are reading this meditation on Ash Wednesday, the day that ushers in Lent. Lent offers both a remembered and an anticipated journey to those who set out on its observance. Lent remembers those narratives in the Gospels where Jesus and the disciples slowly but decisively make their way toward Jerusalem. The recollections recount unexpected and unfamiliar terrains encountered on this journey: the teachings of a Messiah who suffers and dies, the betrayals of a right-hand stalwart, the adulation-become-accusation of the crowds, the beloved of God executed in a way associated with those accursed by God.

The *anticipated* journey of Lent involves the way we journey today toward the passion of Jesus in Holy Week. We make this journey in solitude and community. Consider how you will make that journey in this season. Perhaps you will participate in midweek suppers and studies. Perhaps you will give up or take on some personal spiritual discipline. This book will accompany you in the coming weeks of Lent.

As you begin the journey through Lent with this book as both portal and path, you may find yourself asking the same question raised by those first disciples: "Why do you speak . . . in [*write of*] parables?" Parables speak indirectly, so it seems we only overhear their storied narrations of other persons, things, or places. Wouldn't it be more useful just to "tell it like it is," to be straightforward and plainspoken? Give me a list of disciplines to do. Explain what Lent means. Tell me the requirements of discipleship so I can understand it and live it. Amen to all of those goals! Yet for those very reasons, the parables of Jesus guide this Lenten journey. Why?

The answer lies partly in Lent as a *remembered* journey. No single biblical narrative of Jesus' journey to and passion in Jerusalem has not been known and duly publicized for nearly two thousand years. Depending upon your longevity in the church, you may have traversed the Lenten path any number of times. Easter Sunday, like Good Friday, will come as predictably as the first Sunday after the first ecclesiastical full moon after the spring solstice that sets Easter's date. Jesus' itinerary on this way has all been spoken and heard before. Yet because the parables of Jesus provide metaphors for what this journey means rather than minute details of its schedule, they offer a unique way of reexperiencing its passion. They invite our imaginations as well as our memories to envision anew what Jesus reveals about God and the coming realm that lies not only

? vernal equinox?
not "solstice" sun stand still

ahead of us but within us. Is not the point of Lent to rediscover what God reveals on a cross and through an emptied tomb?

The answer to "why parables in Lent" goes back in part to my friend in the opening story. Traditional religious discourse simply does not click for some folks. In my friend's case, insight came through use of words and images with which he was familiar. Jesus' parables use the language of everyday life and experience, not religious code words learned through lifetimes of religious study. In other words, parables invoke the language of the mundane to depict the inbreaking of the holy.

Some interpret Matthew 13:10-17 as saying Jesus used the indirect speech of parables so that "outsiders" wouldn't be able to understand. When we read the passage closely, particularly verse 13, we can make a strong case that Jesus' aim is the opposite: to enable understanding and hearing not currently happening. Listen to the way Eugene Peterson in his translation *The Message* renders a portion of that verse: "That's why I [Jesus] tell stories: to create readiness, to nudge the people toward receptive insight."

Parables nudge us *all* to receptive insight. For those new to the Lenten journey, they give access to the holy through the ordinary. For those who have navigated this season many times, they allow an opportunity to experience Lent from a different perspective. Jesus' parables go beyond chronologies of what happens. They take us deeper, revealing the approaching realm of the God who has come to us in One who teaches still in parables.

Open my spirit, O God, to see and hear, to receive and understand, the revealing of yourself to me this day and these coming days of Lent, through the parables. In Jesus Christ. Amen.

SPIRITUAL EXERCISE

If you are able, attend an Ash Wednesday service today. If that is not possible, reflect on how you will observe this season of Lent in solitude and in community.

SIMPLE GIFTS

*W*hen casting the meaning of God's sovereign realm in parables, Jesus does not turn to arcane symbolism accessible to a limited few. To a culture closely connected to the earth, Jesus speaks through the ordinariness of seeds and vines. To individuals who kneaded bread and swept floors, Jesus offers images of God's purposes in yeast and misplaced coins.

The simple nature of these parables' objects reminds us that the sacred often dwells in the common and ordinary—and is just as often overlooked. Jesus' life shares that characteristic with his parables. The very incarnation of God passed largely unrecognized in our midst (John 1:10-11). The vision of human spirit, like that of human eyes, sometimes remains sadly superficial. A mustard seed is a mustard seed is a mustard seed. Nothing more.

The simple elements of the parables press us to look deeper into these ordinary elements used by Jesus to reveal the sight and nature of God's realm. We look deeper into the ordinary elements of our lives attempting to glimpse God's purposes. We look deeper into the ways we use the gifts of God and to what ends.

Remember the destination toward which Lent moves. On Good Friday, simple gifts of wood and iron crucified the one who taught in parables. When we do not see the sacred in life, we may lose sight of the sacredness of life.

Look, then, this week with eyes and spirits wide open to ordinary things and common persons . . . and the One who teaches that God's realm may be seen in the simplest of gifts.

WHO WOULD HAVE EXPECTED?

The Mustard Seed   *Mark 4:30-32*

The time had come to plan the annual Christmas pageant at the small Methodist congregation I served. In recent years the girls chosen to play Mary had been a series of high-achieving young women from the congregation. One had been a state dairy princess. Others had excelled in school athletics or 4-H competitions; they all had their turn.

This year Joanie's turn had come. Joanie did not have the eye of the high school coaches who kept watch over their flocks for up-and-coming point guards or spikers. Those who knew Joanie best at school were special education staff who worked with the developmentally disabled. Lois, who had planned the pageant over the past several years and whose daughters had served their turns as Mary, talked with me about Joanie. Lois's good heart believed it would not be right to pass Joanie over. We agreed, understanding the pageant just might be different this year. It was.

Actually, the pageant itself did not prove much different from others: a few missed lines, the children could have sung a little louder, an awkward silence or two. The difference came in its epilogue. After the final scene, the children left the front of the church to join their parents while the liturgy moved on to a candlelit reading and song. The one glitch occurred when Joanie, instead of leaving the baby Jesus doll in the manger, carried him with her as she took a seat in the front pew below the pulpit. It would have been clumsy for me and embarrassing for her to go down and get the baby Jesus to put back in the cradle for all to see. So I continued the service, resigned to having an empty cradle at the center of the Christmased sanctuary. It was not until the lights went down, however, that I noticed what no one else could see. The light that illuminated the pulpit area leaked to that first pew. There sat Joanie in the near dark, holding and rocking that doll with the gentleness of a mother caressing her own child.

Who would have expected Joanie to be the quintessential Mary? Perhaps the only one not surprised that night was the One who first taught the parable of the mustard seed.

A mustard seed represented figuratively, if not literally, the smallest of seeds. Those who pay attention to such details place the diameter of a mustard seed at 75 thousandths of an inch. In other words, the mustard seed is easy to overlook—and easier yet to dismiss as holding no significance or potential. Yet the parable asserts enormous potential in spite of all appearances. The significance of that potential is not merely growth into the "greatest of all shrubs" but the resulting shelter that nurtures life "so that the birds of the air can make nests in its shade."

Some have interpreted this word of sheltering as alluding chiefly to the inclusion of Gentiles in early Christian community. While that remains an intriguing possibility, the force of the parable's ending moves us toward other considerations. Namely, where do we experience the need to extend such hospitality and shelter today? How might we evidence God's coming realm, which Jesus likens not only to a mustard seed but a mustard plant? Answers specific to your congregation and your individual discipleship go beyond the scope of this book. But using this parable for direction, we look for folks who need a place of shade. Be attentive to those whose bodies and spirits, without the shelter of community, might be left vulnerable in a world only too eager to let others fend for themselves. And then—this being the tricky part—offer such nurturing community that embodies the gracious hospitality of God's sovereign realm.

At this point the parable makes its strongest connection with the season and movement of Lent. Jesus practiced this parable. He gathered to himself as followers not a who's who of all the movers and shakers of that era but those at the margins: women, fishermen, tax collectors. In the shade of his discipled community Jesus sheltered one who denied and one who betrayed and a host of others who fled into the night. And the way the Gospels speak of it, Jesus extended such hospitality knowing full well what would come of it . . . and what would come of them. Jesus did so with trust in a vision of God's coming realm that relied on mustard seeds: mustard-seed disciples, who barely registered on the radar screen of faith at the outset and even when matters came to a head at Jerusalem and Golgotha. Mustard-seed apostles, who within a generation, sowed seeds of hope and birthed sanctuaries of community all the way to Rome.

Mustard seeds remain the birthplaces of the gospel and the stirrings of our own spirituality. There is no word of grace too small, no act of love too insignificant, no individual or community of faith too unimportant that does not bear within it the seed of God's coming realm. I read that in the parable of the mustard seed. I saw that watching Joanie cradle the baby Jesus, sheltering for all of us the gift of Christ's coming.

Holy God, surprising God, open me to the ways and to the ones that bear you to me. In Jesus Christ. Amen.

Spiritual Exercise

Look around the room to find some small, easily overlooked item. In what ways does that item contribute to your life or to the life of others? How might it be like a mustard seed? Offer a prayer of thanks for such small, overlooked blessings in your life. Pray for an individual or group, easily overlooked, in need of shelter and welcome. Consider ways in which you might be an instrument of hospitality.

Above All Else

Hidden Treasure   *Matthew 13:44*

In 1988 a building contractor in Oregon received a small inheritance from a family estate. Among the items was a small collection of Lewis and Clark memorabilia. Amassing Lewis and Clark books and material quickly became the man's obsession. He sold his home and maxed out several credit cards to pay for acquisitions. In a lot of eyes he played a fool's game. As the start of the Lewis and Clark bicentennial drew near in 2003, he sold his collection to a university for many times over what he had paid. He has since retired, draws a comfortable annuity from investment of the sale, and devotes himself full-time to pursuing his interest in the Lewis and Clark expedition. "'The kingdom of heaven is like treasure hidden . . .'"

Pious readers of Jesus' parable of the hidden treasure might object to such a crass comparison. We could argue that the Lewis and Clark devotee acted recklessly. He put himself and whoever depended upon his livelihood at great risk. Did not Jesus himself teach the hazards of laying up treasures (the same word as in the parable) on earth versus treasures in heaven?

It is well that the parable of the treasure occurs early in this book, for it highlights the tendency of parables to go beyond face value. The individual in Jesus' parable who finds the treasure illustrates that unsettling truth. For example, just what was he doing, prowling if not digging around in somebody else's field? His problems become more complex once he finds the treasure. Should he not have gone to the owner? Instead, the individual hides it *again*—as if to keep it from the owner's attention. The individual then goes and buys the field. But does he really own the treasure? The rabbinic traditions on such matters are mixed at best. Many conclude that the weight of such arguments falls on the side of the original owner's retaining rights to the treasure.

Morally speaking, this parable raises more questions than it answers. But then, like another parable in praise of an unjust steward, Jesus does not tell this parable to teach ethics. He tells the parable to reveal something of the sovereign realm of God.

What that "something" is connects to another story in Matthew's Gospel—not a parable but an encounter with Jesus (19:16-22). A promising young man comes to Jesus, asking the question that drives all seekers of God: "What must I do?" Jesus' answer to the young man mirrors the parable's core revelation of God's realm: nothing else can compare. All else is secondary. Pay any price. "Go, sell" are the hard words of Jesus to this young man, the exact same verbs this parable uses to describe the actions of the finder of treasure. The dilemma for the young man is his treasure. Yet Jesus extends the promise to him: "You will have treasure in heaven." A gift that has been hidden till now from this individual's life is uncovered. But unlike the character in the parable, this young man walks away from the treasure, grieving.

The parable of the treasure confronts us with the priority of God's realm in our lives. It challenges seekers and followers of Jesus to evidence such unrivaled primacy in the ordering of our lives in the light of that priority. Nothing else can compare. All else is secondary. Pay any price. Those words do not rest easily in societies or congregations where "moderation in all things" may serve as the byword for enforcing conformity and preventing obsession. Moderation in all things cannot understand, much less tolerate, people who sell all they have to obtain a treasure they may or may not legally possess. Moderation in all things cannot understand, much less accept, someone who sets his face toward Jerusalem knowing what will unfold there.

The problem is that the gospel of Jesus Christ incarnates the immoderate. In this parable an individual finds hidden treasure that launches an obsessive shedding of all encumbrances in order to obtain that one thing valued above all else. God's realm is not to be simply one of many coequal pursuits in our lives. Its grace brings the gift; its call brings the summons to reorient the whole of our lives and communities in its light.

"'The kingdom of heaven is like treasure . . .'" Is it really that way in our lives? Is God's realm the one thing we treasure above all else that motivates who we are and how we do things? Is God's realm the one thing above all else that pries loose and lets go of what we have for the sake of its gift beyond measure? We may still find such treasure. And when we find it, the treasure may still beckon us to holy obsession.

Holy God, instill in me such seeking of your grace and presence, such practice of your love and forgiveness, such working for your justice and peace that treasures you. Amen.

Spiritual Exercise

List the five items or persons you value most highly in life. Beside each entry, note (1) the reasons for that valuing and (2) the practical ways in which you express that valuing. Consider now how those reasons and expressions compare to why and how you value faith and your understanding of what is meant by "the kingdom of heaven." Read Matthew 13:44. Be at prayer about the priority that faith and God's realm have in your life compared with other values. Be open to the Spirit's grace and challenge in your treasuring.

TENACITY

Lost Coin   *Luke 15:(1-3) 8-10*

A woman loses one coin. Big deal! How many of our sofas are laden with dimes and quarters that have slipped out our pockets? Our advice to the woman might be, get over it.

Some commentators have similarly belittled the value of that one coin in order to emphasize her searching as a lot of effort for something quite insignificant. Others look at it differently. A silver coin was in that day's economy the equivalent of a day's wage. Think about what you make, before taxes, in a day's time—or what your monthly retirement check divided by thirty would come to. I suspect that sum, if misplaced, would encourage your searching. Or consider this: the woman has ten coins and loses one. In the days before CDs, annuity funds, or federally insured savings accounts, those ten coins might represent the totality of her savings; she has just lost 10 percent. Again, think of your own savings, pension accounts, or nest egg. If you lost 10 percent of your total assets, would you shrug it off as just one of those things and move on? No, like that woman, you would likely sweep with tenacity through records and receipts in order to find out where it went.

Tenacity. The dictionary in my office notes that the root of *tenacity* in Latin means "to hold fast." That definition leans slightly in the direction of stubbornness but with a difference. Stubborn people dig in their heels to avoid movement for fear of change. Tenacious people keep their feet and hearts in motion in hope of holding on to or restoring something they value.

Determination in relationships arises because we see and know the value of those persons in our lives, our families, and our churches. Tenacity means we do not find it easy to let go of folks we hold dear. In churches this resoluteness often comes into play in the ways people rally around those who are ill and in need of support. Faith communities can become persistent in caring for others by cooking meals, staying in touch, running errands. My son's god-mother entered the final stages of terminal cancer, and most members of her congregation at a small Methodist church in south-ern Oregon became hospice volunteers, caring for her and her husband in every way possible. They tenaciously tended to life, even in its ending.

Life, and with it the experience of joy, marks the direction of Jesus' parable—the joy that comes in finding, after tenacious searching, the joy in the heart of God when one who has been lost becomes found. Such joy enriches our lives. Sometimes we miss joy because we busy ourselves too much in the routines, whether at home or in sanctuary. Tenacity helps us hold on to the experience of joy intended in those relationships. The determination revealed in this parable originates in what God has done in our lives. In the end the parable suggests that above all else is the resolute love of God. The parable envisions God as this housecleaner who sweeps her home and searches carefully until she finds that valued coin. We learn tenacity in the very grace of God for us, grace that is our joy and our hope.

As we learn tenacity from God, this parable invites us to put it into practice. The church is strengthened when we actively value others and remain open to one another in times of disagreement. Likewise, God invites us to put such persistence into practice in our family relationships by determinedly valuing other members and not giving up on one another in times of conflict.

Another sort of stick-to-itiveness looms just under the surface of this parable. Luke prefaces it and the parable of the lost sheep with a word concerning audience. Jesus' keeping company and table fellowship with sinners has galled the righteous of his day. Luke 15:3 says, "So he told *them* this parable" (emphasis added). Them who? The sinners, the ones who could all too easily identify with things that were lost and the joyous surprise of being sought out and found? Or the righteous, the ones who may have found it difficult to empathize with this woman's action or joy?

The tenacity of Jesus' ministry in general and this parable in particular addresses and seeks both insider and outsider. The parable may speak differently to each group, but it includes both. That point is worth remembering as we follow Jesus' journey through these parables toward Jerusalem. There is a tenacity to Jesus' movement and words: even when warned, he will not turn back. But there is also a determination to Jesus' seeking of folks from across the spectrum of standing before community and God. He speaks with love to a rich young ruler. His words shelter an adulterer about to be stoned. He dines with Pharisees and tax collectors.

Why? For the sake of joy that comes, as with this woman, in the finding of any and all who were once lost.

You search me out, O God, with tenacity for the experience of joy—yours, mine. And so you search out those most unlike me. Teach me such grace and its exercise in my seeking. Amen.

Spiritual Exercise

Reflect in your journal on an experience where you exercised tenacity in a relationship. Note your motives, the difficulties involved, and the joy that may have resulted. As a recipient of God's determined searching, consider your life. In what ways have you experienced that persistence? In what times have you known the joy of being found by grace and forgiveness? Hold on to those experiences with thanksgiving, accepting them as encouragement to exercise grace toward others with tenacity.

Hidden

In the past several years a number of people have asked me how I came to be a writer. I can point with clarity to significant moments in that process. I can name with precision professors, editors, and colleagues who provided decisive help or opened doors once closed. I marvel at the succession of links that speak less to me of coincidence than of serendipity.

But what I find most amazing in hindsight are the ways this transition in my life and ministry has largely been out of sight and awareness. My deeper thinking on how this came to be draws me to things and preparations hidden at the time. I did not know then how valuable diagramming all those sentences on the blackboards of Baden and Walnut Park elementary schools would be. I did not fully appreciate then the encouragement, not to mention discipline, of Mr. Bernard and Miss Weiner and especially Miss Enright to read good literature back when schools were not intimidated from having reading lists. I did not realize that preparing a sermon from week to week over the years (and Sunday does come with surprising regularity!) would transform a card-carrying procrastinator into a born-again believer in deadlines.

These and other experiences gradually, imperceptibly, yet powerfully made it possible for that change in ministry from parish work to writing to occur. At no time in those early years did I consciously perceive how and why those elements worked as they did in hidden ways. Even now I would not venture to claim that the instruction of my teachers and the discipline of sermon writing was merely to prepare me for what I do now. Each of those things and others I do not have the time or recognition to single out had a value in and of itself in its own time. But what I do say now, for only now do I see it, is that this remarkable congruence has been working all along in hidden ways to ready God's fresh working in my life.

The parable of the leaven reveals a like understanding and trust. By its own preface, the parable focuses on the nature of God's sovereign realm. "Three measures" of flour represents approximately eight gallons, an impressively large amount that will be influenced by a small addition of leaven. Leavening would take time, the dough being set aside in a warm and dark place. The parable underscores the hiddenness of God's unfolding realm through use of the verb translated by the NRSV as "mixed in with." The verb *egkrypto* literally means "to hide or conceal."

That concealment seems painfully clear in the times in which the church lives, now as always, between promise and fulfillment. We yearn to see signs of justice, mercy, and compassion among us. We long to witness and embody the qualities of God's realm in the midst of powerful contradictions and oppositions to their way. To look on the mass of creation and history at face value might lead to resignation or despair. The parable pushes us deeper, pushes us to trust that all of those tentative beachheads of grace and almost imperceptible advances of goodwill come to fruition. It is a parable of hope and encouragement.

And in its assertion of God's workings deep within a creation and a history that seems so flawed, the parable addresses individuals and communities who would take its light as their own. I spent so much time dealing at this reading's outset with hidden workings in my life, not to set myself apart but to invite your own identification with this parable. I say without fear of contradiction that God has been and continues to work in hidden ways to bring renewal to your life. You may already perceive some of those ways. Some still await your discovery. Grace continues to leaven who we are with what we may yet be. We may be unable to put our finger on it or define it or say "that's it," but we may trust God's unseen influence.

One final word: in Jesus' day leaven was created through the process of rot and decay. As a result, leaven often symbolized religious corruption. Paul used the image of leaven to indict moral laxity weakening the church (1 Cor. 5:7). Jesus used the figure of leaven to denounce the corrupting influence of misleading religious authorities (Matt. 16:6).

This parable's signifying the influence of God's realm through leaven would have been a scandalous thought in its day, contrary to conventional thinking. Keep that in mind through this Lenten journey. What Jesus is about in the movement of this season does not always match conventional thinking or traditional piety. The influence of God on Jesus' way to Jerusalem is much like leaven: not immediately perceived but hidden away in words and actions whose meanings will not become clear until later. Even when a cross comes into view and noises of betrayal and silences of desertion come into play, God will be at work in hidden ways like a woman leavening flour in preparation for loaves eventually to be broken.

> *Leaven my life, O God; leaven this creation with your presence. May I then not only trust but act on the preparations you make for my life and all life. Amen.*

SPIRITUAL EXERCISE

Reflect on where you are now in your life of faith. Spend time considering ways and persons who have, in hidden ways, brought you to who you are and what you do in Jesus Christ. Offer prayer for your openness to the Spirit's leading, for a willingness to consider how God has been preparing you for opportunities and challenges that feel like they are just around the corner. Trust God's leading in your becoming a new creation in Christ.

Vine and Branches   *John 15:1-5*

"I am the vine, you are the branches." Technically speaking, Jesus' words here are not considered a parable, but their metaphor of life lived in connection with Christ serves a parable-like function in signifying spiritual truths in elements commonplace to that era.

Much writing about vineyards and vines in biblical times deals with harvest or pruning nonfruit-bearing branches to encourage growth in those on which grapes have formed. Pruning and harvest do stand large in this metaphor. But notice that the main assertion has to do with vine and branches. Before productivity determines pruning that eventually leads to harvest, there is a vine and its branches. What defines the nature of the relationship between these two involves the verb Jesus uses no fewer than five times in these verses in the English of NRSV: abide. *Abide* translates a Greek word that means "to dwell" or "to remain." Abide describes the sense of connectedness between vine and branch.

Connections. Those with backgrounds in electricity and Methodism will bring particular understandings to that word. In electricity connection refers to a place of contact between two lines that determines whether a wire will be live or not. I can only speak of the Methodist understanding of connection from afar, from several years as an O.A.D. pastor (Ordained in Another Denomination, not D.O.A.). In my experience I heard folks speak of connection as the link between Methodist bodies ranging from local congregations through districts to conferences on to quadrennial assemblies and international bodies. Connectionalism serves in that language as does "covenantal community" in other traditions, including my own. But whatever phrase we wish to adopt as an institutional byword, the underlying truth we hope to incarnate in our relationships is this notion of "abiding" together in Christ.

"I am the vine, you are the branches." Think about the branches of a vine, perhaps one that grows in your yard or a park you visit. My thoughts run to a wisteria vine by our patio and two grapevines just outside our back door. What stands out about the branches in my estimation is this: how much alike they are. They may shoot off in this direction or in that; they may have differing numbers of leaves. But when I look at the wisteria branches on our trellis or the grape branches on the cedar post fence, I am struck by how closely they resemble all the other branches on that vine. The branches are not differentiated in terms of one type being the sunlight-seeking ones and another being the growing-out-of-the-vine ones. They are pretty much the same.

Who we are in Jesus Christ, when you get right down to it, is pretty much the same. Now I have preached my share of sermons on Paul's imagery of the different parts of the body of Christ and how all those differences intend to complement the whole. But Jesus in the Gospel of John seeks to make an alternative point from Paul in Corinthians. "I am the vine, you are the branches" dwells on this radically democratizing notion that life in Jesus Christ comes down to this critical connection of branches with the vine. The parable or the metaphor, however you name it, urges this core understanding that every branch is alike in its need for connection to the vine. Connection (abiding) with Christ serves as the bottom line of who we are and how we live and what will become of our efforts to be fruitful. We all draw our life, our mission, our spiritual mooring in that connection with Christ.

Now just at this point trouble may arise. Some branches on the vine may speak up and say, "That's right! We are all alike. If any of you differ from me (and I know I am living in Christ), then you need to change or face pruning." Some branches draw that line or propose that pruning "cut" on the basis of church polity, charismatic behavior (or the lack thereof), politics, or inclusion of others deemed unworthy. But listen to the parable: "I am the vine, you are the branches." Friends, branches are branches—no one of them is the vine. What gives us life, what holds us in living relationship with God, is not engrafting ourselves to another branch. Fruitfulness does not derive by being cloned in the image of another branch or insisting others replicate how we do "church." Fruitfulness comes through maintaining that unique and vital point of connection with the One who joins us to the Holy in our midst. "'Abide in me'" (verse 4) implies we have a choice: Will we abide in the vine named Jesus?

"I am the vine, you are the branches." Winter approaches as I write these words. The leaves on the grape branches have nearly all dropped off, and the wisteria will soon do the same. More than ever the branches come into view, as well as those places of connection with the vine from which the branch derives life and fruition. Seasons come and go in our lives. The foliage of spiritual journey changes through our times of turning as well. But what remains, what abides, is that place where our lives join to Christ. In that place we find ourselves connected in this time for all time to God.

Join my life to you, O God, in ways ever deeper and ever stronger. And may my living draw from you the hope and love that renew and transform me ever more in your image. In Jesus Christ. Amen.

SPIRITUAL EXERCISE

Imagine yourself a branch on a vine. Visualize how you draw life and stand through wind and bear fruit through your connection to the vine. Imagine your life joined to Christ. Name the ways you have drawn life from that relationship and found strength to weather storms and borne fruit in the service of Jesus Christ. Offer thanks for that connection.

STUDIES IN CONTRAST

*O*pposites attract, so the saying goes. But opposites can also reveal. Drawing contrasts between two candidates for office, so long as we focus on authentic differences and not false smears, offers one of the best ways to reach a decision on voting. Drawing contrasts between two perspectives on art or two styles of writing may guide students or practitioners of either to hone their own skills.

Drawing contrasts also serves as a familiar tactic in the parables of Jesus explored in this chapter. We view insights into God's sovereign realm through the prisms of particular individuals. Some are named by common relationship (two sons) or status (two debtors). Others are paired at the outset by what sets them apart (Pharisee and tax collector, rich man and Lazarus). In one case Jesus draws the contrast within the same individual (rich fool).

Studies in contrast form a natural choice for teachings regarding God's realm. Distinct differences separate the qualities dominant in this age and those characteristics evoked by God's coming realm. Studies of contrast also lend themselves to the season of Lent. The movement toward Jerusalem and discipleship draws sharp differences with conventional wisdom urged by the powers that be in this or any age. *Life is to be seized for the sake of survival, not risked for the sake of community. Power and wealth are to be held at all costs rather than expended on behalf of others. Say what you please, but do what you want.* Listen to these parables as they contrast such understandings with images of community, humility, and richness measured in love set to deed.

As Good as Your Word

Two Sons   *Matthew 21:28-32*

Judy, my wife, tells me the garbage sack under the sink has gone beyond tolerable limits. Would I please take it outside? Over in my lounge chair, feet propped up, watching TV, I say, "Fine, I'll get to it." She's happy to hear that. The next morning she opens the cupboard door. The garbage sack still brims full to overflowing. Words alone don't take out the trash.

Our son currently counsels youth at a juvenile detention center. As part of the treatment, the program guides a youth in taking control of some part(s) of his life that contributed to incarceration: anger, an inclination to act first and think about consequences later. A not infrequent response during the course of treatment will be a confident, "Don't worry; I'm not going to get messed up with that stuff again." Several months later the same individual returns to the center. When "that stuff" presents itself, the attraction proves too great. Saying no in treatment is only half the battle. Acting and living the answer out on the street proves the more revealing response.

Jesus' parable of the two sons touches on an ongoing struggle for many: saying what other people want to hear rather than what we intend to do. Maybe the one youth in Jesus' story knows his father will be upset if he says no to his request, so he tells him yes and then does nothing about it. The story does not psychologize the episode. We do not get a childhood development lesson from Jesus. The story does not explore whether this has been a pattern slipped into early in life, perhaps encouraged by parental permissiveness and a lack of follow-through on earlier promises. As intriguing as such thoughts might be, the parable totally ignores them. It focuses entirely on this one exchange: the child *says* yes but *does* no.

The contrast occurs with another son. The parable actually begins with this child who says no but then changes his mind and does yes. Again the parable does not tell us all we might like to know. Did the child see the look of hurt or anger in the face of the parent and thus change no to yes? Did momentary distractions cause someone used to saying yes to, in this one instance, say no? Those are not Matthew's interests, nor are they apparently Jesus'. What matters is the doing of the word, a theme that stretches all the way back to the sermon preached from a hillside that opened Jesus' teaching ministry in Matthew ("Everyone then who hears these words of mine and *acts on them* will be like a wise man . . ." [7:24, *emphasis added*]).

Words alone don't take out the garbage, nor do verbal assents constitute faith. The force of the parable insists on change. Words point us in the right direction and describe possibilities for action. Words inform others of our good intentions and confess God's good gifts. But even the best of words risk irrelevance if they do not find themselves matched with enactment and incarnation.

And if the truth be told, individuals and communities of faith sometimes fall into the trap of trying to go on word alone. Worship can become a show of words made entertaining and mystical in their appeal but disassociated from what goes on outside the hallowed walls and stained-glass windows and PowerPointed screens of our sanctuaries. Confessions of faith can become battlegrounds over adjectives and images that distract our attention from dying children and warring neighbors. Mission statements can become overgeneralized paragraphs that, in trying to say everything, say nothing. In the process they may take time and energy away from the literal meaning of mission as being sent out for action.

Do not misunderstand me or the parable. Words are important. Creation issued from the word of God ("And God said"). Redemption took form first in incarnation (the Word made flesh). But words take their importance, as revealed in those narratives of creation and redemption, by actions that enact love and that fashion community and embody grace. The youth in the parable who said no at first does not model how we should speak. What the parable insists on is that he does provide example for how we may act. Even when we get the words wrong—and the best of us will do that from time to time—grace makes it possible for us to get the action right. We may change. We may turn.

If you seek example of this in Lent, look no further than Peter. He begins by saying yes ("I will not deny you"). But then his actions and words betray ("I do not know the man"). If that were the end of the story, Peter would be left on the outside looking in, along with all the self-righteous paragons indicted at the parable's close. But Peter's yes then no eventuates in another yes made possible by extraordinary grace: "Simon son of John, do you love me?" . . . "Yes, Lord; you know that I love you." God honors and Spirit empowers change, change revealed in the conduct of lives transformed by the grace of Jesus Christ. For in Christ even our no can become yes.

Gracious God, shape my trust of you with integrity of word and deed. And when my words fail, or I fail them: speak to me, restore me, renew me in word and deed. In Jesus Christ. Amen.

SPIRITUAL EXERCISE

In your journal write down the "words" you find most difficult to keep. Pray for insight that understands where and why you balk. Pray for renewal in acting as you speak and as you believe. Write down the "words" or affirmations most important in your faith journey. Offer a prayer of thanks for their gift to you and for the grace of God that works in your life through them.

"I" Disease

The Rich Fool   *Luke 12:16-21*

"The land of a rich man produced abundantly" (12:16). The linking of *land* with *rich* in the parable's opening underscores this individual's wealth. Some folks can be land rich but cash poor. Others can be landless but affluent. This person has it both ways. His prosperity multiplies with a bumper crop. Parts of the Hebrew Scriptures attest to the belief that material and spiritual well-being go hand in hand. Modern proponents of the so-called health and wealth gospel make a similar case. In such eyes the individual in the parable appears blessed of God.

But appearances, like possessions, can deceive. Listen to the parable's words. "What should *I* do, for *I* have no place to store *my* crops. . . . *I* will do this: *I* will pull down *my* barns and build larger ones, and there *I* will store all *my* grain and *my* goods. And *I* will say to *my* soul." The nouns and pronouns tell the story: *I, I, my, I, I, my, I, my, my, I, my.* Self-interest serves as the *only* interest. Have you ever been around someone like that? Then again have you ever been someone like that?

The original crisis in the parable had been an overabundant crop. What do you do with all this stuff? It is an interesting problem, but it is not a problem new under the sun. In Genesis 41, Egypt faced a similar dilemma. Seven years of plenty filled Pharaoh's storehouses to overflowing. What should Pharaoh do? Buy a couple more villas on the delta with the added cash flow and live high on the hog while the living is easy? In contrast, Joseph advises storehouses for the surplus to insure the community's life, not just Pharaoh's prosperity, during the ensuing lean years. The storehoused harvests provided sustenance for the community's survival, not windfalls for individuals to hoard as much as they could collect for themselves.

Therein lies the connection with Jesus' parable. In the Hebrew Scriptures bountiful harvests embody God's saving intentions for community. On the surface it might seem that the man in the parable acts no differently than does Joseph: both are storehouse builders. Actions, however, turn on motives. Joseph's storehouses fill with grain to sustain the community through famine. The parable's projected storehouses intend to rise as monuments to this man's self-indulgent enjoyment. All of those *I*s and *my*s betray the man's ultimate plan: "'Soul, you have ample goods laid up for many years; relax, eat, drink, be merry.'" It will be a paradise on earth.

But it is a fool's paradise. Of all the things that we can store, life is not one of them. "'You fool!'" God interrupts. "'This very night your life is being demanded of you.'" *Fool* is a loaded word in the wisdom tradition of Israel. Fool refers to those who live as if there is no God. The identity fits the man in the parable, not because he is stupid or moronic but because he lives oblivious to God and oblivious to those around him. Foolishly.

"'So it is with those who store up treasures for themselves but are not rich toward God.'" Accumulating wealth is not necessarily the problem: the crunch comes in the *use* of wealth. That is why this parable continues to address those who would follow the parable-teller. We are persons of wealth. Few of us may enjoy the windfall of this man in the parable—although those who live in places like Somalia and the slums of Calcutta might make a formidable case that we do. But even if we distance ourselves from extravagant prosperity, the truth is that all of us have wealth at our disposal. All of us. And regardless of the degree, the principle applies: the use of wealth poses a choice between wisdom and folly. The parable speaks to us.

Positively stated, the parable's message comes in Jesus' final three words: *rich toward God*. In the original Greek manuscripts *rich* is not a noun in this sentence but a verb. "Rich toward God" takes *action*. Rich toward God suggests how we direct our wealth, how we use our resources. Whether we are rich toward God is not limited to a once-a-year ritual of deciding how much we give the church next year. Rich toward God summons an expansive vision of how you and I use what we have for the sake of others: church included but not exclusive. Rich toward God includes neighbor and stranger, family and friend, society and church. Our practice of rich toward God takes its cue from God's richness toward us in creation, in redemption.

In the parable, the individual's obsession with *I* and *my* stands in sharp contrast to other words of Jesus spoken at his very turning toward Jerusalem. "'If any want to become my followers, let them deny themselves.'" Self-denial need not be reduced to self-hatred, although the church has sometimes fallen into that abusive trap. Self-denial, as revealed in the parable of the rich fool, simply rejects the self as center of the universe. Self-denial, as revealed in the parable, just as significantly invites life that is rich toward God and the community sustained by God's providence. Only in the midst of community can self-denial be practiced as we know ourselves to be graced and valued by God.

> *Save me, O God, from self-interest divorced from community good, from self-denial separated from the command to love neighbor as self and you above all. Amen.*

Spiritual Exercise

Reflect on the phrase, "rich toward God." What does it mean to you? Make a list of your five most important material possessions. What makes them valuable to you? Consider that list in tandem with "rich toward God." In what ways does such richness influence the way you view and use those possessions? Pray for guidance in living with such richness with your resources.

Do You See?

The setting opens innocently enough. A Pharisee named Simon invites Jesus into his home for dinner. Or perhaps it's not so innocent. Table fellowship has become one of the sticking points between some religious leaders, including some Pharisees and Jesus. Should Jesus sit down with a would-be opponent? Refusing to eat with those who have strict rules against dining with sinners might leave Jesus open to the charge of practicing a reverse prejudice.

That remains a tricky issue to navigate. How do we maintain ties to those with whom we disagree? One option demonizes them so that we have nothing to do with them. The course of politics and some church squabbles point to that as an increasingly preferred strategy. It's difficult to sustain reasonable dialogue, for example, among those of polarized opinions on abortion. One side reduces the other to baby killers, while the flip side charges antiwoman rhetoric. Meanwhile, the middle erodes. Some in the church demonize the Pharisees as Jesus' archenemies, a judgment that has fomented centuries of anti-Semitism. Jesus, apparently, doesn't agree. He sits at table with Simon.

The dinner party goes haywire from the outset. The reason? Architecture starts it. Seriously. Few homes then have doors with locks. If the evening's warmth or the cooking fire's smoke congests the air in the room, the doors will be left wide open to the street— open for the breeze and who knows what else to blow in. The text records Jesus' taking his place at table. That doesn't mean he pulls up a chair and sits. Custom dictates reclining for the meal.

So picture the scene: door wide open to the thoroughfare, host and guests reclining around a table. And then it happens. That is, *she* happens. What her name is, the text gives no clue. What her identity is: well, the euphemism used is "a woman in the city." From that, many identify the woman as a prostitute, though the text does not make that explicit a charge. The woman, victimized by her reputation in this town as a sinner, tends to suffer from the between-the-lines implications of the text as well. The intricate way Luke weaves this story entices us to make the same assumptions of gossip that pilloried her in the first place. Maybe Luke does that to remind us just how pernicious and enduring gossip can be.

From this point forward the woman dominates the dinner party. Jesus' reclining at the table makes it much easier to visualize her ensuing actions: bathing his feet with her tears, drying them with her hair, kissing his feet and anointing them with oil. Her actions disgust Simon. Polite host that he is, he keeps his thoughts about Jesus' unprophetic behavior to himself.

Jesus does not. His thoughts take the form of this parable. Two debtors owe money to a creditor: one debt equals almost two months' pay, the other closer to one and a half years' wages. Neither person can pay the debt. But the creditor cancels the debts. So who, Jesus asks, will love the creditor more?

Jesus makes an odd connection. You'd have thought Jesus would have asked, "Who will be more grateful?" Or, "who will feel more indebted?" But for some reason, neither gratitude nor IOUs interest Jesus. "Which of them will love him more?" Simon mouths the right answer. "I suppose . . . "

"I suppose" does not exactly convey conviction. So Jesus comes at Simon from a different direction. "Then turning toward the woman, [Jesus] said to Simon." "'Do you see this woman?'" Jesus asks. That is one way to avoid persons and situations that cause us discomfort. We just don't see them. If homeless folk trouble us, don't look at them. If conflicts in families or churches distress us, don't acknowledge them. But the world doesn't work like it did when we were three or four years old. Then we could squeeze our eyes shut, and what we didn't want to see would disappear. Not anymore. "Do you see this woman?"

Jesus insists that Simon see her, because she answers the parable's question of who loves more. She, more than Simon, has proved hospitable. A good host provides water for the washing of the guest's feet, soiled and worn from traversing roads of dirt and rock in sandals. But Simon provided no water. A good host greets the guest with a kiss of friendship. But Simon offered no kiss. A good host brings oil to soothe the guest's head and hair from the burn of sun and drying of wind. But Simon provided no oil.

For every act of hospitality that Simon neglected, Jesus looks at this woman and says to Simon, do you see her? Do you want to see forgiveness embodied in love, because here it is. Here *she* is. "Which of them will love more?" the parable asks. And Jesus' answer? "Do you see this woman?"

Jesus has an odd way of making heroes out of the most unlikely of characters. Samaritans, parents who forgive prodigals—and here, an unnamed woman whose utterly humble actions show love's origins not in moral certitude or religious acumen but in forgiveness. A self-righteous Simon forgot about hospitality. The church might take note there of what happens when we forget to make ourselves and our communities hospitable places to those whose need of forgiveness simply reminds us of our own. The church might also take note of what happens when forgiveness unleashes love.

"Do you see this woman?"

O God, grant me eyes and spirit that open to your grace and to the ones you grace, that I may learn from them and from your forgiveness bound together in love. Amen.

Spiritual Exercise

Whom do you have difficulty accepting or even looking at? Pray to see them as Christ sees them. Pray to see yourself as Christ sees you. Forgive and be forgiven. And seek to love.

PROVE IT!

Rich Man and Lazarus *Luke 16:19-31*

Have you ever played a game called "Prove It"? It's not a board game or video game. You can't order it from Milton Bradley or Nintendo. It's one of those games we play in relationships, adaptable to all ages. Children often play it. "If you think you can climb the tree as high as I can—*prove it!*" Sometimes it has a darker side, used to exclude someone who is on the outs at the moment. "If you're really my friend, you won't play with Robin—'cause I don't like her." As children mature, the game gets more sophisticated. The love of parents becomes the target of the testing. "If you really loved me, you'd trust me and let me stay out later."

And adults? A substance abuser has no qualms about demanding that loved ones cover for his or her problem. "If you really loved me, you'd call my boss and tell him I'm sick." An abusive parent or partner will play the same game, asking silence about the "secret."

"Prove it" has two major problems in human relationships. It is a game that can be very destructive, used to distort even the best of qualities for purely self-seeking ends. In the name of love or friendship, some very unloving and unfriendly behavior seeks justification. The other problem is its addictive nature. In relationships dependent on "proof" of love or friendship, the demands for proof never go away. Like any other addiction, spiraling degrees of proof are required as time passes. Relationships based on constant proofs fight a losing battle, because in the end love or friendship must derive from trust. And trust is not something you can coerce from another person. It will be learned through experience, not proved by contrived tests.

This notion of trust versus proof goes to the heart of Jesus' parable of the rich man and Lazarus. The parable opens with a study in stark contrasts: a rich man who enjoys the benefits of this world's elite, and Lazarus who has to raise his eyes just to see past the gutter. When the next world comes, everything turns upside down. Beyond a morality tale about how tables get turned (and they will!), Jesus moves the story in an additional direction.

The rich man offers up what seems a hint of compassion for others, something clearly absent in his previous ignoring of Lazarus. The rich man (in some traditions called Dives) asks that Lazarus be sent to warn his five brothers about the follies of their ways. The appeal seems reasonable. It would be like the scene in *A Christmas Carol* by Dickens, where Ebenezer Scrooge's long-dead partner, Jacob Marley, visits him. The sounds of Marley's chains, forged by long years of greed and indifference, begin the journey of Scrooge toward compassion and humanity.

But listen to the reply of "Father Abraham" to Dives, a response that returns our focus to the theme of proving. "They have Moses and the prophets; they should listen to them." But the rich man is not satisfied. "But if someone goes to them from the dead, they will repent." *Bible, Schmible—nobody pays attention to that anymore. But let old Lazarus show up on the doorstep, and my brothers will beat a path to you. That'll prove it!*

Or will it? Abraham appears to be well accustomed to the game of prove it and its tendency to always raise the stakes. "If they do not listen to Moses and the prophets, neither will they be convinced even if someone rises from the dead."

In the context of the parable, these words sternly reject the game of "prove it" when it comes to faith. One does not negotiate with God over the terms of faith. Faith is rooted in a relationship of love. Love is not something to be proved but trusted.

Beyond the parable these closing words become even more intriguing. The parable is told by Jesus: Jesus who later resuscitates a friend by the name of Lazarus, Jesus whom God resurrects to life at story's end (and discipleship's beginning). Does the parable's conclusion teach that even those events cannot prove faith? The answer may surprise us. The resuscitation of Lazarus pivots John's Gospel.

From that point forward the Temple authorities determine Jesus must die. Capital punishment, not faith, is the verdict of the raising of Lazarus.

Jesus' resurrection evokes similar results. Disciples dismiss the first Easter witness announced by the women as an "idle tale" (Luke 24:11). Jesus shows his wounds to Thomas, only then to bless those who will believe without seeing. "If they do not listen to Moses and the prophets, neither will they be convinced even if someone rises from the dead."

Faith cannot be proved by apparitions from the dead any more than it can be verified by an alleged burial shroud subjected to scientific scrutiny. Proof is not and never has been the point of our life and standing in Jesus Christ. Rather, faith beckons trust expressed in love.

Save me, O God, from endless bargaining and proof-testing of your love. Deliver me into the grace that sets me free to live with grace and to trust you wholly. Amen.

SPIRITUAL EXERCISE

Consider your faith and participation in faith community. Where do you struggle with the need for proof? How does the need for proof affect your ability to trust in God, in others, in yourself? Pray for guidance and discernment in these matters. Seek a more gracious trusting of God with your life, relationships, and faith community involvements.

Whom Do You Trust?

Pharisee and Tax Collector   *Luke 18:9-14*

The story is told of a nobleman in Victorian England who commissioned a portrait photographer to take his picture. The man suffered no lack of self-esteem, coupled with an overly optimistic view of his attractiveness. The photographer brought his equipment to the gentleman's home and proceeded to set it up in the parlor. All along the noble felt no qualms about offering unsolicited advice to the photographer about his preparations. When all was ready at last for the photograph to be done, the noble announced: "Young man, mind you to do me justice with that camera of yours." With hardly a pause the photographer responded, "Sir, your need for my camera's work is not justice but mercy."

Jesus tells a story to a group that suffers no lack of religious self-esteem. Two individuals pray at the Temple: a Pharisee and a tax collector. The Pharisee comes to the Temple, not so much imploring God's acceptance as declaring his fitness for it. The prayer of the Pharisee thus becomes not a baring of his soul but a review of his resumé. Grace is not really needed, much less asked for, since the Pharisee mentions ample evidence for his standing with God being obvious to everyone—including God. "'God, I thank you that I am not like other[s].'" This Pharisee is not like the extortioners, the unjust, the adulterers, to use the words of the parable. To put a more contemporary spin on it, this Pharisee is not like the ones who spend all their time in the bars or the welfare cheats or the Aryan Nations wingnuts. The prayer of the Pharisee, in ancient or modern dress, requires no divine presence. It only needs an audience of those who share the same disdains and the same upright behavior for the sake of self-congratulation.

The second prayer partner in the Temple is a tax collector, a traitorous parasite who exploits his own people by collecting the taxes of a foreign occupier. He stands back in a corner where he won't upset anyone with his presence. Scarcely daring to raise his eyes off the floor and with a gesture of despair, all he can pray is, "'God, be merciful to me, a sinner!'"

According to Jesus, the tax collector—not the Pharisee—returns home justified in God's sight. As Jesus saw the matter, everyone who sets himself or herself up will be taken down a few notches, while those who humble themselves will be exalted. "A person's pride will bring humiliation, but one who is lowly in spirit will obtain honor" (Prov. 29:23).

Justification looms large in the parable's close as the most definitive distinguishing point between these two individuals. What separates them at the end are not the obvious variances in lifestyle, piety, and social stature (or the lack thereof). One returns justified; one does not. And the one who does catches us off guard and unprepared for the choices God makes.

But even justification does not exhaust what lies at the heart of this parable. The Pharisee and tax collector engage in no dispute about who justifies. They both go to the Temple and offer their remarkably different prayers to the same God. No, a question other than who justifies drives the text and our own encounter with this parable. And that question is, Who do you trust? The parable tips its hand on this focus at the outset: "[Jesus] also told this parable to some who trusted in themselves. . . . " The parable addresses those who seemingly have every right to feel justified. Its telling then and its hearing now confronts individuals and communities (and nations) whose prayers resemble announcements to God of, "Mind you to do me justice with that camera of yours." Then and now, the parable challenges individuals and communities (and nations) whose prayers exalt their standing because they are better than others. For "better," you might substitute richer, more powerful, smarter, more godly. "'God, I thank you that I am not like other people . . . even like this tax collector.'" For "this tax collector" you might also substitute "those Muslims, those fundamentalists, those liberals, those secular humanists."

By comparing ourselves to others, particularly in ways that stack the deck in our favor, our prayers and spiritual posturing may reveal that we trust more in ourselves than in God. Or it may reveal a diversion on our part to avoid facing our own brokenness and fears. Either way, as long as we can find someone worse off (in our estimation) morally, spiritually, or politically, we risk seducing ourselves into thinking we stand justified in God's sight. Haven't we just proved that? But justification does not come down to showing how fortunate God must be to have friends like us. Justification turns on whom we trust. To trust in self is self-justification. To trust in God, even when the trust comes from a lowlife like this tax collector, opens us to God's justification.

It is a scandalous parable, and the name of the scandal is grace.

May I see myself as you see me, O God, that I may trust my true self to you. Wholly. May I see others as you see them, O God, that I may accept them as you accept me. Graciously. Amen.

Spiritual Exercise

In your journal reflect on places of your life where you have difficulty trusting: trusting other persons, trusting God. As you are able, identify sources or causes of that difficulty. Pray about those matters that hold you back from trust, especially those that might have to do with a reluctance to share your true self or admit to weaknesses. Imagine the hands of God cupped open. Place yourself in that space held up by God. Entrust yourself to God.

Week Three

ATTENDING TO CREATION

*P*salm 19 asserts the heavens' witness to God's glory. Jesus directs us to flowers of the field for a lesson on life without anxiety. This chapter's parables invite our attentiveness to creation for discerning the movement and meaning of God's realm in our midst.

Paying heed to creation reminds us that we exist as individuals of flesh and blood. We live with feet planted on earth, with eyes and ears intended to take in sights and sounds, with noses breathing in an array of scents ranging from honeysuckle to human sweat, with tongues savoring favorite foods and tasting the salt of tears. God fashioned us in connection with the created order, and we find in creation signs of God's purposes and grace.

To ignore or, worse yet, to abuse creation comes with costs. We deny our God-bestowed identity as creature and blind ourselves to creation's witness. We use up bounties intended for renewal over the passing of generations into whims that suit the voracious consumption of a single generation. We risk employing the good gifts of God's handiwork for unnatural purposes. Thorns that once adorned vine and blossom go pressed into a forehead. Timbers that could have been shaped into furniture instead frame the killing utility of a cross. The passion and suffering of the Christ still linger when creation goes abused in any such way.

Listen then to these parables of creation. Through them listen to and honor the earth, sky, and air—all of which bear the mark of God, all of which God entrusts for the sake of life. God still speaks through creation, if only we take the time and care to attend its gift.

RECEPTIVITY AND EXTRAVAGANCE

Sower and Seed   *Mark 4:3-9*

Judy possesses the green thumb in our family. Gardening and marriage proceed on an even keel so long as she keeps things simple for me. Take planting, for example. I wield the shovel. When she says dig, I understand the only knowledge I need is, how deep?

But they say a little knowledge is a dangerous thing. And I do possess a little knowledge about soils. I grew up near the confluence of the Missouri River and the Mississippi. The floodplain of the Missouri in that region is extraordinarily flat, even for the Midwest. One of the main avenues going through that area near my childhood home was called Missouri Bottom Road. During the normal spring floods, that land and often that road were literally at the bottom of the river. But that land, that dirt, was also the richest in the region because the flooding replenished the soil. Bottomland was good land. Good dirt. Fertile soil.

"'Listen! A sower went out to sow.'" The only character in this parable is a sower, a farmer. The only action of this individual is to scatter seed. It is a one-dimensional parable—at least, in the beginning. Not until one gets past sower and seed does the drama, the uncertainty, and the surprise of the text come into play. And those aspects derive not so much from the sower and the seed as from the soils upon which those seeds go scattered.

"Some seed fell on the path. . . . Other seed fell on rocky ground. . . . Other seed fell among thorns. . . . Other seed fell into good soil." Now for some of the practical among you or at least those with farming or gardening experience, you may begin to wonder what was wrong with this farmer. Why didn't he take more care in the planting of seeds in the furrows, which would maximize their chance for germination? This individual seems rather reckless, tossing seed to the wind as if he doesn't care where it lands.

Scholars debate this very point. In some places in first-century Israel, plowing preceded planting. A more careful approach to sowing probably would guarantee a higher rate of return. But in other places seeding came first and then plowing. Wherever seed landed, it would be tilled into the ground—or crushed in the process. So is this sower following normal methods for the day, or is he extravagant to the point of excess? The lavishness of the sowing, even on places that seem to hold no hope for life, offers a glimpse into the extraordinary grace of a God who brings shoots from dead stumps, receives prodigals with open arms, and risks the ninety-and-nine for the sake of one lost sheep.

Such extravagance on the part of the sower comes up against the receptivity of the soils. Hard paths and rocky ground allow no entry, no deep rooting. The story of Jesus' visit to his hometown of Nazareth comes to mind. There, Mark tells us, Jesus could do very little in the way of miracles or acts of power. Any number of conditions can cause hardness. Familiarity can stifle acceptance, as in the case of Nazareth. Hard and fast assumptions can rule out the potential of anything beyond what we presume to know or experience already. Too much grief, too much sadness can crust spirits against hope. Too much wealth can calcify hearts against compassion for those who are without. Arrogance can shut the door tight to any interest beyond self-interest.

Receptivity is key: in the garden, to the gospel. God does not batter down the doors we hold tightly shut in fear of whatever. God invites and beckons, sowing grace with reckless abandon—but God does not bully us into faith. God waits and hopes; God works in unseen ways but in ways that respect our creation as persons with response-ability.

But when we open ourselves to those word-seeds of gospel and God's realm, remarkable things may happen. For the extravagance in this parable is not only in the sowing but in the harvest. Thirty and sixty and a hundredfold are the parable's expressions for what may issue from receptive soil. We have no idea, once an opening is given to grace, where it will lead and what it will result in: in our lives and multiplying out to others. Five loaves and two fish fed multitudes. The single life of Albert Schweitzer literally brought healing to thousands of others.

"'Listen! A sower went out to sow.'" Even if just one seed falls on receptive ground, growth will come. So Jesus sowed words extravagantly across the hillsides of Judea and the shores of Galilee, on the likes of those who fled into the night when it came to arrest. Jesus even sowed words on both Peter and Judas, in hope that the gospel might find a receptive spirit. Maybe not immediately but eventually. So the word still goes sown extravagantly *among* and hopefully *by* us—for we cannot presume to know who will or will not respond.

"Listen!"

Loosen those hard and brittle places, O God, that scale over my ears and my spirit. Open me to the grace you would sow in me and through me. In Jesus Christ. Amen.

SPIRITUAL EXERCISE

Get a handful of potting soil or other dirt that would be good for planting seeds in. Note how it feels: its looseness, its dampness, its texture on your fingers. Prayerfully consider how your life "feels" as soil in which God's word of grace is sown. How might you become more receptive to receiving and living that grace?

RISK

Lost Sheep   *Luke 15:4-7*

A huge body of literature and analysis is circulating these days; it goes by the name of "risk aversion." What is it? Mathematically, "an agent is 'risk-averse' if $C^u(z) \leq E(z)$ or $\pi^u(z) \geq 0$ for all z M" (http://cepa.newschool.edu/het/essays/uncert/aversion.htm). If you are like me, however, that only muddies the waters. Economically, "risk aversion" has to do with how much risk you are willing to put up with or pay to avoid when it comes to decisions about investments or business strategies. Those who speak in such tongues categorize folks as risk averse (*I'm not going to chance it*), risk seeking (*don't you just love not knowing what's going to happen*), or risk neutral (*I don't care if it's risky or safe, I'm going to do it*).

A Google search on "risk aversion" this morning revealed 1,210,000 hits on the topic; that number rises daily. Apparently people these days have a high interest in risk and its aversion. I will not presume to tell you that I searched through every one of those entries. In the few I did, I encountered theories and illustrations whose orientations leaned heavily toward the mathematical and economical in nature. But I never found a single theological example. And that is too bad, because Jesus posed an intriguing story about risk aversion to the church, a story even more intriguing when read in the risk-tinged season of Lent.

"'Which one of you,' Jesus begins, "having a hundred sheep and losing one of them, does not leave the ninety-nine in the wilderness and go after the one that is lost until he finds it?'" To me that is a loaded question. Sometimes we avoid its implications by thinking Jesus only asked it of a group of tax collectors and Pharisees almost two thousand years ago. But the truth of the matter is this: when Jesus says, "which one of you," he truly and pointedly means "which one of us?" Which one of us would take that shepherd's risk? And it is a risk. Jesus doesn't say the ninety-nine get left in the protective shelter of the sheep pen with other eyes to watch and other hands to pick up the work that has been set aside. The ninety-nine get left in the wilderness, out in the open, exposed to the dangers. Which one of us would risk 99 percent of what we have or value or love for that 1 percent that has gone and gotten itself lost?

The answer is not automatic in churches. Which one of us would be overjoyed with a pastor who goes off and ignores the need of ninety-nine members and spends way too much time trying to reconnect with that one whose feelings got hurt or whose judgment got impaired and who now never darkens the church door on Sunday morning? Which one of us would be willing to see the church's ongoing and traditional ministries to the overwhelming majority of members suspended so that time, energy, and resources can be risked in an attempt to reach that one small percent of folks who don't currently respond to what we do around here?

The answer is not automatic in families. Which one of us would be willing to risk the stability, if not security, of family members who are dutiful and diligent for the sake of trying to connect with the wanderer, the one who never has really fit in—and with no real guarantee of finding, much less returning? Which one of us would be willing to cast love time and again to the same bad seed who ninety-nine times out of a hundred will disappoint or lash out in return?

We do this parable a terrible disservice to presume that the shepherd's action is standard operating procedure. We need to keep in mind that in this era shepherds were seldom the owners of the flock. They were hired hands sent out to care for somebody else's property. Put yourself in the place of that owner when the shepherd comes back, "Well, sir, I've got good news and bad news. I went out on a limb to find one lost lamb—and I got him! 'Course, I should tell you that while I was gone, the other ninety-nine got eaten by wolves. But I've got the one!"

This shepherd needs to learn a lesson about risk aversion, we'd think. *Risking all that flock just for one? Doesn't that individual know it's better for one to die than for the whole nation, er, flock to perish?*

That is the problem with Jesus, you know. He doesn't get it sometimes. Jesus makes it seem like that one wandering lost sheep has just as much value as the whole flock put together. Or that those sinners and tax collectors amount to the same in the sight of God as decent and upright people who can recite Torah or catechism blindfolded. Jesus needs to take a course of study on risk aversion. Because if you keep taking risks, you're going to get burned—or crucified.

That is the problem with following Jesus, you know. Discipleship is not, in the parlance of our age, risk-averse. Why else would we listen to someone who once said that those who want to save their life will lose it? And why else would Lent intentionally lead us to Jerusalem?

Which of us would follow a shepherd who embraces such risk?

That you would set all else aside for my sake and my finding,
I give you thanks, O God. That I would risk for the sake of
others and their finding, I seek your grace, O Christ. Amen.

Spiritual Exercise

Reflect in your journal on times and ways in which you have engaged risk or avoided risk in your practice of faith and discipleship. What allowed you to risk? What held you back? Consider now where you are in life and on your spiritual journey and one particular issue where a decision involving risk may be before you. Pray for God's guidance in that matter. Seek to discern how you may choose and act—not recklessly but graciously.

WEEDS, FOXGLOVES, AND POTENTIAL

Tares among Wheat   *Matthew 13:24-30*

I occasionally preach at the Lutheran church in my town. One Sunday the vase on the altar was filled with light purple blooms running down long green stems. The organist remarked not only on its beauty but the fact that many folks consider foxgloves to be weeds.

Jesus tells a story about a wheat field where weeds sprout up among shoots of grain. It is interesting that the first question in the parable is not *What shall we do?* but *Why did this happen?* "Master, did you not sow good seed in your field? Where, then, did these weeds come from?" There is more to that question than meets the eye, for lurking among those unsown weeds is the question of evil in the world. God is good. God created the world. So whence comes evil? Philosophers have danced around this question ages long without any ultimate answer that ends the questioning.

But you don't have to be a philosopher to ask this question. Not too many years past, I attended the funeral of the four-year-old son of friends in the community. They were a devout and hardworking couple just starting to take over the dairy owned by the dad's parents. But shortly after the birth of one of their sons, the child began to exhibit signs of liver failure. Four years later we gathered for his memorial. "Master, did you not sow good seed in your field? Where, then, did these weeds come from?" Personal illness, business crisis, family breakdown: in a variety of settings, for any number of reasons, we understand the dismay of the servants. We want to know how weeds infested our gardens. We want to know that if God is good, then why this?

The initial answer given by the householder in the parable simply says: "An enemy has done this." The weeds are not the doing of the householder, the sower of the wheat. The weeds have the fingerprints of an enemy. What that response leaves unanswered is *why* that householder—why God—has let such a thing happen.

Weeds infesting a grain field is bad enough. But the suffering of innocents in tsunami-devastated southeast Asia? The onset of cancer in a child? "Master, did you not sow good seed in your field? Where, then, did these weeds come from?" And if the answer is that an enemy has done this, then why allow an enemy that opportunity? The parable really does not attempt to answer the age-old wrestling over the existence of evil. Instead, Job-like, it accepts the task of living faithfully in the face of mystery. How does one live in a world where weeds do infest the ground, and evil does rear its head in powerful ways that defy pat answers?

One tactic that suggests itself immediately involves getting rid of the infestation. That is where the servants in the parable see the conversation headed. "Do you want us to go and gather [the weeds]?" "Search and destroy" is this solution to evil. Got a problem with weeds? Pull 'em up. The church employs this strategy in many quarters. Got a problem with sinners in the church? Throw 'em out. Got a problem with abortion clinics? Bomb 'em. And on and on we might go . . . except for other considerations.

For one, who determines what (who) deserves eradication in the church, not to mention society? For centuries, and with biblical texts to back it up, folks who loaned money at interest were called usurers and severely castigated. Now our economies thrive on usury. Churches are urged to develop endowment funds, pastors to invest in pension funds that depend on collecting interest on money owed. I once heard something about people who live in glass houses. . . .

An even more compelling argument against the search-and-destroy approach to evil arises from the parable. When the servants ask about going out to weed, the householder replies, "No; for in gathering the weeds you would uproot the wheat along with them." From a distance, search-and-destroy might seem the most effective method, but it falls short. Why? For the sake of innocents who might fall victim in the process. In this parable the householder values wheat above all else. He will go to extraordinary lengths to protect the grain from, in the current language for such things, collateral damage. The destruction of weeds is not worth the suffering of the wheat.

It can also be hard to distinguish weeds from wheat in our lives. Roots may be too closely joined. The grace of God's potential may not be clear. Consider John Newton, who captained a slave ship for years, bringing many into the misery of slavery. Some might have considered an early death for him a blessing for the world. Yet Newton's later transformation moved him to compose the words of "Amazing Grace." Imagine the loss had Newton been "weeded out."

The parable asserts rightly that God is a different kind of farmer: different because God's love of the wheat is so absolute that even weeds will be tolerated until harvest, so as not to uproot the beloved. That love may not answer all our questions about why the weeds, the suffering, the evil persist. But that love does guide the way we live in the midst of a thorn-infested world. Knowing we are so loved by God, we are called to so love others—even those whom our first judgment dismisses as weeds. Sometimes what we take for a weed ends up a life of beauty and faith before God . . . like those foxgloves on the Lutheran altar.

I thank you, O God, for grace that did not uproot me when I showed more signs of sin than faith. Teach me to exercise such patience in the potential of others, even my enemies. Amen.

Spiritual Exercise

Journal about a time in your life when God might easily have given up on you but did not. How is your faith different as a result? Pray for someone you find it easy to give up on. What potential might you be overlooking? What forgiveness might you extend?

PRODUCTIVITY AND GRACE

Barren Fig Tree   *Luke 13:6-9*

A barren fig tree. On the surface you might suppose this parable is much ado about nothing. Rare would be the owner of such a tree who was able to hire a caretaker if only one tree comprised his holdings. The tree is likely but one of dozens or hundreds in a vineyard. And rarer still would be the owner whose vineyard grows for purely aesthetic reasons. Fig trees produce figs. Therein resides their value. That is their purpose. And if one tree is not producing, it is taking up valuable space. Something has to be done, and we understand why. Take it down. Get another. Move on.

Except . . . except when you scratch the surface of this parable, the situation is not quite so mundane as it may appear. Take fig trees, for example. Their role in Hebrew life and thought is more than dietary staple, though it was that. Over time the fig tree came to symbolize God's shalom, the peace that goes far beyond the absence of conflict to the presence of all that makes for wholeness and richness of life. When Micah sought to depict what life will be like in the restored Davidic commonwealth, he wrote, "They shall all sit under their own vines and under their own *fig trees*, and no one shall make them afraid" (4:4, emphasis added). The fig tree stood as a vital symbol of God's blessings upon Israel. The fruitful fig tree represented the faithfulness and responsiveness of God's people to such grace.

But a *barren* fig tree? Barrenness cuts two ways in the traditions of Hebrew scripture. It came to be popularly understood as a levying of unfavorable judgment by God. To be barren was to be cursed, emptied of promise and future. Yet, precisely out of that tradition, barrenness came to be the fertile working ground of God's unlikely grace. God transformed the barrenness of Abram and Sarai into the child they named "laughter." Hannah's tears became cries of joy at Samuel's birth. Jesus' own cousin, who came to prepare his way and who warned of axes being laid to the root of trees that did not bear good fruit (Luke 3:9), was born to a couple deemed barren. So mention of a fig tree without fruit, barren, cannot be heard apart from both of those traditions. By the grace of God, the fruitless may yet become fruitful.

The owner, as we might expect, did not come with grace on the tip of his tongue. A tree is only as good as its fruit—and if this one's not going to produce, let's get another in here that will. But the gardener's approach differs. The owner looks at trees and vines from far off, on an account sheet. But the gardener is, in the literal meaning of the Greek word, "one who *works* a vineyard." The worker's hands touch plants and earth. If there is cutting to be done, the worker's hands will be the ones that will have to wield the ax. So the gardener says, "Not yet. Let me do a little more work. Fertilize the ground. Loosen the soil. Give some extra care. Another year."

It doesn't make sense, you know. Figs produced fruit after three years. So it is likely this tree has already had at least three years to grow. And a levitical proscription about the first three years of fruit from a fig tree being unclean might even suggest the tree may be six or more years old. Why would you check fruit you couldn't harvest? But however you determine the age of this tree, it clearly is barren. The owner has logic and practicality on his side. And the gardener? Parables have a peculiar way of making God- or Christ-figures out of the truly unexpected ones. As Luke will later speak of a father who acted with Christlike love toward a prodigal, so this parable portrays the grace of God in the reluctance of this gardener to do anything too hasty. This hands-on worker allows more time to see if a miracle might yet come, if the barren might still produce fruit. And who knows, the parable's impression might suggest that when the owner returns next year and sees no fruit, then this gardener might make the case for just one more year and one more and one more. . . .

At what point must productivity and fruitfulness sway the day? After all, Jesus has just spoken twice in this chapter about the need for all to repent, the need for all to align life and spirit and ethics to the coming reign of God. But even that summons serves as an extension of God's grace. God seeks fruitful lives of those who follow, but grace prepares and precedes whatever we do with a love that has already accepted us for who we are.

Fruitfulness is our response to God's reign, not our entry fee.

Gracious God, you know my desire to be fruitful. Remind me of your grace that patiently loosens the soil around my intransigence and lovingly works and coaxes me into life. Amen.

Spiritual Exercise

Prayerfully consider places in your life and faith that may have grown barren of late. List them in your journal. Ask God's Spirit to lead you toward renewal and fruitfulness in those areas. Confess what may be holding you back. Accept God's grace that makes fresh starts possible. Visualize that grace as working to loosen the earth around your faith's roots, letting in more nourishment to energize and transform you. Offer God thanks for the patience of grace and the promise of Spirit.

NAMED AND FED

Good Shepherd   *John 10:1-5, 11*

There is a power in names and in knowing names and in knowing ourselves named. Our first naming comes in our families, but it does not end there. Individuals may gain nicknames, by which and sometimes for which they are known. There may be vocational or professional "namings" that shape how others see us. In the church in which I grew up, it was years before I ever learned that Pastor Prell actually had a real first name. And on more than a few occasions, the conduct and sometimes the language of others has markedly changed when someone mentioned that I was not simply John but also "Pastor Indermark."

The parable of the good shepherd points to the importance of names and knowing ourselves named. The goodness of this shepherd concerns more than the assertion of sacrificing one's life for the flock. Before that, goodness comes revealed in the trust of those who know themselves named by that shepherd. In Hebrew and Greek, the languages of scripture, the word for shepherd literally means "one who feeds." The function of shepherds, as the word implies, involves feeding the flock entrusted to their care. "Entrusted" is key, for shepherds rarely owned the flocks they tended. They were hired to feed, nurture, and protect the flock.

In the parable the sheep follow this good shepherd—not because he holds the biggest staff but because they know his voice; he calls them by name, and the sheep trust him. To be known by name and to know trust is no small gift in this world. We may take it for granted when we live in places and among persons for whom we are part of the landscape. But travel to a place far from family and friends, from colleagues and acquaintances, and you will likely discover what a gift it is to hear a familiar voice. And sometimes those travels that take us where we are not known or named are not measured in miles or kilometers but in journeys of the soul. Have you ever found yourself in a place where it seemed no one truly understood you, truly knew who you were beyond superficial acquaintance? Worse yet, have you ever lost sight of yourself? The death of a loved one, estrangement from a partner, addiction, depression; there are an abundance of places where we may long to be known and need to be fed, named. Shepherded.

I have strong memories of Christmas day 1974. I was in the middle of my intern year at a church in Portland, Oregon. I did not have the finances to make a trip to St. Louis for the holidays, and this would be the first Christmas in my life I had spent away from home and family. It promised, or maybe the right word is *threatened*, to be a lonely time as only holidays can exaggerate loneliness. But anxiousness turned to promise when Jopel and Elizabeth shared their family's Christmas with me. The mix of generations, the food, the singing, the genuine sense of joy in that house (not to mention Elizabeth's Bavarian Christmas crème nog): that day, I was fed and named, shepherded.

In the parable the good shepherd "calls his own sheep by name and leads them out." In doing so, the parable invites us to listen for the voice of Christ in our lives. It encourages a listening that enables us to follow, a following that the season of Lent reminds us will at times bring us to places we might not have chosen on our own. But I also hear this parable beckoning reflection on how we name others and what our voicing of those names brings. Oftentimes the voice of Christ will seek human form—and human "shepherds." What names do we call one another by, in addition to the names announced at baptisms or that county clerks put on birth certificates? Are they the voices and sounds that engender love and respect or fear and resentment? Are they names that build and nourish our identity as family members and as human beings, feeding our spirits in a way that brings healthy growth? Or are they names that cut and ridicule, depriving emotional sustenance and stunting growth?

Think of the word we sometimes use in the church with the ritual of naming: *christening*. The name we receive literally intends to leave us—and lead us—"in Christ." In Christ we, the beloved of God, know ourselves named by God's love. In Christ the Good Shepherd we trust ourselves to the leading of the one whose voice we know, the one who lays down his life for the sake of the flock.

In this year's journey that is Lent we move one day closer to that sacrificial aspect of Jesus' ministry for our sake. Yet always, always, we move as those who know we can trust this voice with our very lives. For we move as those who know we are named by such a love and led by such a shepherd.

Holy God, you are the one who knows me wholly, the one who names me and feeds me with grace. So I may follow you, so may I trust you. Wholly. Amen.

Spiritual Exercise

In your journal, list the names by which you are known in life (such as daughter, friend, Judy, family surname). Reflect on what those names bring to you and how they feed you. Note your thoughts beside each name. Think now of the names that God bestows on you. How are you known to God? How are you fed by God? Offer a prayer of gratitude for all the ways in which God names and nurtures your life. Seek God's leading for what it means to live as one who has been named.

RESPONSIBLE RELATIONSHIP

*T*he first epistle of John asserts that "those who say, 'I love God,' and hate their brothers or sisters, are liars; for those who do not love a brother or sister whom they have seen, cannot love God whom they have not seen" (4:20). That is a startling word about the potential and responsibility of life lived in relationship with others.

Little wonder then that when Jesus crafts parables to speak of God's realm, human relationships form a frequent and revealing context. Many of the parables already considered in this book have drawn upon elements of human relationship and responsibility. So we do not break entirely new ground in this chapter.

But what may surprise us in the parables now considered are conflicted examples of our relations with one another. Four of these five parables put characters at the center who are described as unjust, unmerciful, or unclean. In the fifth, folly as much as wisdom provides for Jesus' revealing of how life is in God's sovereign realm.

Perhaps this is as it must be. If Jesus had been limited to perfect cases of human interaction, we might still be waiting for a parable to be spoken. That we do not yet live in God's realm fully realized means we may need to catch glimpses of its coming in this less-than-perfect world and our own less-than-ideal interactions.

So these parables in their own peculiar way offer hope. Even in relationships whose fullness too often eludes us, even in responsibilities kept only with reluctance if at all; even here, even now, we may perceive God's realm. And in that perception, we find it possible to trust with hope, to act with responsibility, and to love God through loving those with whom we stand in relationship.

Foolish Assumptions, Wise Preparations

Wise and Foolish Bridesmaids   *Matthew 25:1-13*

An A-frame building rises at the edge of the Paradise flower fields at Mount Rainier National Park. It houses a mountaineering guide service. Groups regularly gather there for guided ascents. Even those who tackle the peak without a guide check in for the latest weather conditions.

The climbers one sees by that building are impressive. They are weighed down by huge packs that seem to be stuffed with a week's worth of supplies, even though the climb is a one-night venture. Ice axes, crampons, ropes, all lashed to the pack frame, resemble an old-time tinker packing a store on his back. Anything that might be needed has to be packed. The cost for preparedness comes in the weight felt in every burning breath and each knee jolt on ascent and descent. But the price for assuming one can climb unprepared is deadly and too often exacted.

Assumptions about many things in life can have disastrous results, especially when they lead us to believe we don't need to exercise foresight. Such assumptions wreak havoc in the parable from Matthew. The setting for this story is a Middle Eastern wedding. Remnants of its customs continued into the more remote Palestinian villages. The bridal party awaits the bridegroom at the home of the bride's parents. Most of the wedding guests wait there as well. However, it's the responsibility of the bridesmaids to escort the bride out to meet the groom when he comes. From there they join a procession that leads the whole party to the groom's parents' house, where the wedding ceremony takes place. Since this traditionally occurs at night, lamps or torches belong to the procession's ritual. And once again the bridesmaids must be prepared to light the bride's way.

Jesus uses this familiar scene to illustrate his teaching on one aspect of God's coming realm. Five of the maidens he labels as foolish. Why? They take no extra oil for their lamps. They assume no delay in the groom's arrival. They make no preparations in case that assumption does not come to pass. The other five he deems wise because they bring along extra oil. They will be ready if the groom comes on time or early or late. Through these five women Jesus reveals that alignment to God's realm requires actions, not just attitudes, that demonstrate readiness.

Foolish assumptions, wise preparations. What do we make of this parable in our day? Let's start where this parable does: with assumptions. What assumptions do we make of our lives or the church that risk our being ill prepared?

One assumption that affects individuals and institutions is the attitude that life stretches on indefinitely. Some limit this problem to youth who have never had a parent, sibling, or friend die. Death can seem far away in those times, something that only happens to other people, other families. You don't usually think about dying at that age because it seems as if you will live forever.

Adolescents, however, are not the only ones who risk the consequences of assuming life goes on and on. The same foolish assumption can be translated into the primarily adult context that goes by the name of "church." The logic runs something like this. As long as we've been here, so has this church. We have no experience of this church not being here, so we cannot conceive of its not being here. Therefore, no matter what we do or don't do, the church will continue. Right?

Wrong. The church is never a given. Its life never has been and never will be an assumption we can make without need of faithful participation—and wise preparation.

The biblical witness makes clear the danger of assumptions about the indefinite continuity of covenant communities. In times of faith those covenants lead to faithful action, preparing the people for what it means to live in God's presence. Abram followed the call to go. Israel followed the call of Torah. In times of unfaith, however, presuming upon the covenant—and with it, God—leads to the breakdown of relationship, evidenced most clearly in the prophetic explanations of Israel's exile.

The continuing life of faith communities is never a given. It is a responsibility, a trust. The church does not exist merely because it is the church. The church exists to be the church, to do the work of God's called-out people. Wisdom in the church, as in our lives, takes shape in preparing for dynamic partnership with God. Like the five wise maidens in the parable, we do not assume to know all that God will do and when. Rather, God calls us to a faith prepared to respond, however and wherever God may call and seek to work through us.

Lent beckons us to Jerusalem and Gethsemane, to Golgotha and a garden tomb. Do we just assume we have been there and done that before? Or do we prepare for a God who surprises by embodying love, absorbing death, raising life . . . not just way back when but here and now?

Save me, O God, from the folly of presuming to know what I do not know and failing to trust whom I can trust. Help me prepare for you as you are and will be. Amen.

Spiritual Exercise

Journal your recollections of ways in which grace caught you unprepared in God's choice of you or of others. Pray for wisdom in the preparations you sense God seeks for your life this Lent.

LIMITS

The Unmerciful Servant   *Matthew 18:23-35*

A beer company smugly advises consumers to "know when to say when." A parent scolds a toddler whose fingers verge on exploring a live electrical socket. An ethics review board investigates whether a manager's behavior toward a subordinate is acceptable fraternization or sexual harassment. A family wrestles with when to withdraw artificial life support for a dying loved one. What common thread runs through each of these cases? The issue of limits.

Limits we choose to observe determine much of our living, whether legal or moral in nature. Limits set the parameters for our behavior, our ethics, our values. Limits affect how we will live in the most practical of ways. The prelude to this parable voices the same issue. Peter approaches Jesus with a question about limits. Perhaps it rings familiar to you: "How often should I forgive?" When do I reach the limit? Is it, as the old line goes, "fool me once, shame on you; fool me twice, shame on me"? Is it, as the rabbis in Jesus' day taught: three times you shall forgive but no more after that? When Peter asks about extending forgiveness seven times, he has more than doubled society's expectation. But while Peter's guesstimate leans on the generous side, he's not sure. Peter wants to know how many times. And so do we.

So Jesus tells a story. A servant owed a king ten thousand talents. Mathematics helps us understand the grotesque amount of that debt. A servant's daily wage in that era came to about one denarius a day. Six thousand denarii equaled one talent. So ten thousand talents were equivalent to the wages of sixty million work days. To repay the debt this servant would need to work seven days a week, 365 days a year, for about 164,383 years, give or take a century. And that assumes no interest is piling up.

In a pattern the parable will repeat, the debt engenders an act of violence. The man, his wife, and his children are to be sold as slaves. However, a curious turn of events occurs. The servant throws himself before the king, asking for patience. In the height of folly he promises to repay it all. Again, one is drawn to Jesus' humor. You could easily imagine the court of the king bursting into laughter at the servant's impossible proposal. The laughter fades, though, as the absurd promise is answered by an even more ludicrous statement from the king. The king not only releases him; he forgives the debt. The debt is not postponed. The debt is not turned over to a loan officer to arrange a generous repayment plan. The debt is forgiven, cleared. The servant exits that palace without a debt to his name. Or does he?

The freed servant, on his way out, encounters a fellow servant who owes him one hundred denarii. That debt is by no means small, equal to a little more than three months' wages. Normally, that would create some justifiable anxiety. But not today, certainly. Not when the first servant has just received this pardon from impossible debt. However, Jesus' humor in this parable takes a dark twist. The forgiven servant seizes his fellow by the throat, demanding immediate payment. Debt generates violence once more. The beleaguered man makes a plea. It echoes verbatim the request for patience made to the king before, a plea heard then with compassion. The servant, though, hears it with indifference. He has his fellow servant tossed into prison.

This is too incredible. Who could do such a thing? Who could possibly treat another human being that way, having just received such an extraordinary release from debt? The story does not let the scoundrel off the hook. Other servants who witness this injustice immediately inform the king. The servant is summoned and berated for not having dealt with the fellow as he himself had been dealt with. The servant is thrown in jail to be punished (*tortured* is another translation of that Greek word) until the original debt is repaid. Which is to say, in perpetuity.

Jesus' parable literally staggers the imagination because the story constantly stretches the limits so far and so wide. The size of the debt, the mercy of the king, the ingratitude of the servant: every detail is seemingly without limit. Jesus uses that exaggeration to bring us to the story's point. For when the parable seems ended, it is only beginning. Jesus adds this little aside that, if heard properly, takes our breath away: "So my heavenly Father will also do to every one of you, if you do not forgive your brother or sister from your heart." Not from your mouth, not from your enlightened self-interest—but from your heart. God's forgiveness obliges us not merely to gratitude toward God but to forgiving others. It's relatively easy to be thankful to God. The real crunch is offering forgiveness to others, forgiveness that comes from the heart.

A flag of caution is appropriate here. This parable is *not* about accepting continual abuse. Forgiving others the wrongs they do to you does not mean not seeking change in the situation. You can search this parable and not find one word about the king restoring the servant to whatever position enabled him to become so grossly indebted. Contrary to some popular opinion, forgiving is not just another word for forgetting. Forgetting involves a loss of memory, and remembrance is central to faithful life in the biblical witness. Communion is an act of remembrance, including remembrance of betrayal. If we forget those things, we lose the meaning of that meal and its power. Forgetfulness is a vice, not a virtue, of faith.

Because we remember even though we forgive, we are empowered to conduct our lives in different ways. To forgive a spouse for abuse is not the same as forgetting what happened, nor does it necessarily involve returning to that situation. There may be great wisdom not only for yourself but for that other person to do just the opposite. Forgiveness creates the potential for new starts and new life—not the resumption of old ways with unreal hopes.

The parable is clear. God's gracious forgiveness of us is a gift without measure, as enormous as the ten thousand-talent debt of the servant. However, that is not the debt for which God holds us accountable. As with the first servant, our accountability lies in how we respond to others in a forgiving way. It is all too easy to sing the praises of God's grace for me and mine, while holding on tight to a spirit quick to judge and slow to forgive you and yours.

The parable speaks powerfully about such a failure to consider others in the same way God considers us. We are debtors to God's mercy and according to Jesus we are obliged to show mercy. Such are the limits of forgiveness. Such limits are not discerned in asking a numerical response to "how many times do I have to forgive?" No, such limits can only be discovered in asking "how much has God forgiven me?" Then and only then do we discern the means and measure of our forgiving . . . forgiving that comes from the heart.

Teach me, O God, the wisdom and scandal of limits. What I would withhold from another, reveal what you open to me. What I would seek only for myself, remind me of what you offer to all. Amen.

Spiritual Exercise

Recall your past week. With whom in the parable would your words and actions most conform or identify? Why? Call to mind one individual you need to forgive. Pray for the strength and humility to do so. Go and do so in this next week.

For Mature Audiences Only

The Unjust Steward   *Luke 16:1-8*

A colleague of mine once noted that the worship time of many churches runs the risk of being X-rated. His reason was not the presence of excessive violence or explicit sexuality in the liturgy but because worship in some places seemed to be "for adults only."

I have to confess that at times it is just as well the children are not there. For it is true: parts of our biblical tradition will confuse rather than nurture young minds and faith. For example, some texts of Israel's conquest of Canaan tell how the Israelites understood God commanding them to put all the inhabitants of a given town to the sword. Not just the soldiers, mind you, but women, children, elders, even the animals. Read some of the visions in Revelation, of beasts and plagues and all sorts of awful things. Children, by and large, do not possess the background to sort through the wildness of the visions to get to the message.

Parts of our tradition are best left to the mature. While not X-rated, we may think of them as at least PG-13, warranting the presence of a parent, guardian, or trusted Sunday school teacher. Our parable from Luke is an excellent case in point. Indeed, even an adult audience needs to exercise a careful approach, lest we read into it more than it says.

The first word of caution comes in its being a parable. We sometimes read too much into the details of parables, presuming each piece and action must convey spiritual truth. To make that mistake with this parable is to understand why we might cup hands over our children's ears.

The story begins simply enough: a rich man employs a steward or manager to run his business. Word reaches the employer that he is being victimized by white-collar crime, as the manager is accused of embezzling. So the employer summons the manager, confronts him with the rumors, demands an accounting, and gives him his pink slip. The manager perceives his position. He knows himself well enough: he can't survive either as ditchdigger or beggar, and this cushy office job has reached the end of the road. So how does he prepare for the future?

The manager calls in his employer's debtors for a first-century version of "Let's Make a Deal." The first one comes in with a bill showing he owes one hundred jugs of olive oil. Tell you what, the manager says, just between you and me: write down fifty jugs on the invoice. A second enters with a bill for one thousand containers of wheat. No problem, the manager indicates: get out the eraser and change that to eight hundred bushels. . . . Whoa, just a minute! The manager stands accused of squandering the property—ironically, the identical words used in Luke 15:13 to describe what the prodigal son did after he left with his share of the inheritance. But how does the manager address the squandering? By fraud, by cheating, by dishonesty.

The manager's employer returns—the same man who just finished telling the manager he'd heard nasty stories about his malfeasance. Now he's gotten wind of his manager's most recent effort to cover up the mismanagement by juggling the company's books.

At this critical juncture in the parable, let me offer you the opportunity to finish the story Jesus is telling. How would you write the ending? The employer gives the manager a good thrashing? The local courts throw the manager into jail for a long, long time until every penny is repaid? And what message do you draw; wht is the moral of the story you would pass on to future generations about the action of this manager? Two wrongs do not make a right? Honesty is the best policy? Your crimes will catch up with you? These come to my mind. But for Jesus? "And his master *commended* the dishonest manager because he had acted shrewdly" (emphasis added). He commends rather than condemns the fellow. He bestows a commendation on one he acknowledges, even at the end, to be dishonest . . . because he recognizes him as shrewd.

Shrewdness is a word that often carries a negative tinge to it. To be shrewd can imply a ruthlessness in which anything goes to secure the desired end. That is not the kind of shrewdness Jesus evokes in the telling of this parable, anymore than it is told to encourage dishonesty or fraud. What *is* central to this story and its insight about God's realm is the manager's ability to recognize an impending crisis and to plan and act accordingly for the future's sake. As wrong as his particular actions were, the steward prudently and shrewdly assessed his position and acted.

Did Jesus practice what he preached? What would have been the shrewd thing to do when Jerusalem, suffering, and cross came into view? I suggest that the season of Lent reveals that Jesus acted with extraordinary shrewdness. In the face of hatred and accusation he did not look at the immediate crisis and wither. Jesus pressed forward. Jesus acted on behalf of the future. Jesus risked the consequences of faithful action, shrewdly trusting in One who holds all our days, not just the ones immediately upon us. Was that shrewd? Come Friday evening, it looked anything but shrewd. But Sunday morning proved you can't keep a shrewd man down.

Deliver me, O God, to shrewdness, to act as though the whole future depended on this one day's actions and choices. And to live and choose accordingly. Shrewdly. Faithfully. Amen.

Spiritual Exercise

Consider a plan you have for tomorrow or some time in the future. In what ways would faith impact or transform that plan? Shrewdly alter those plans on the basis of your faith.

FAITH AS ABSENCE OR PRESENCE

The Return of the Unclean Spirit   *Matthew 12:43-45*

One theory in logic holds that you can't prove a negative. I believe in some matters that you can't prove a positive with a negative. For example, if we argue that all dogs bark, we couldn't end the debate by declaring that dogs don't meow. That may be true as far as it goes, but it doesn't shed any light on the barking issue. Ethics function on the same basis. We can't prove the goodness of some action (or person) only by observing what it does *not* do. Is Bob a good person? We might agree that the fact that Bob doesn't cheat on taxes is not enough evidence. But would it be sufficient to say that Bob avoids bad things? Does the absence of wrong prove the presence of right?

Consider Jesus' parable of the unclean spirit. Granted, its imagery of wandering spirits in search of unsuspecting human prey may not fit our current views of psychology or religion. It may seem too fantastic, as in fantasy. Remember though that Jesus often framed parables in terms that people, then as now, would find fantastic and unbelievable: servants who owe debts of ten thousand talents (equivalent in its day to the gross national product of Herod's kingdom), Samaritans who are good neighbors, shepherds who risk entire flocks for one lone wanderer. Jesus uses the outlandish to reveal the extraordinary nature of encounter with and response to God. So do not be stopped by the imagery of the parable if you find the details difficult to conceive. Listen for its underlying spiritual dynamic: faith and discipleship need more than what we empty from our lives. Faith and discipleship rely on what fills our lives.

Notice how the parable depicts this individual's inner state *before* the disastrous ending: "empty, swept, and put in order." Two of those words hint at the peril in this state of affairs. "Empty" translates the Greek word *scholazo*. The word literally means "to be at leisure or unoccupied." For the sake of studies, for example, a "scholar" (from *scholazo*) is one who is allowed leisure to focus on learning. For the sake of discipleship, however, a life unoccupied may become a life unfocused. "Put in order" translates *kosmeo*, a word that connotes a sense of beauty and adornment as well as orderliness. And while beauty and adornment are not bad in and of themselves, this verb of "cosmetics" can lead to judgments based on appearances. In another passage, people at the Jerusalem temple commented about "how it was adorned [*kosmeo*] with beautiful stones." Jesus' ensuing declaration of its coming destruction suggests that appearances can be empty deceptions (Luke 21:5).

"Empty, swept, and put in order" do not a disciple make. Yet how often do we limit our examples of and exhortations to discipleship to matters of what we do *not* do. Such a good Christian! Doesn't smoke, drink, or gamble. Doesn't cheat on the spouse or cause trouble at church. Doesn't do this; doesn't say that. All of these attributes can contribute to a good and faithful life; but unless accompanied by more, it can also be a life empty, swept, and put in order. It looks good, but does it *do* any good?

Occasionally parables rely on their context in the narrative to offer further explanation. The parable of the unclean spirit in and of itself doesn't get around to saying what *should* fill our lives in its warning against a spirituality defined only by what we avoid. It is interesting though that the two Gospels (Matthew and Luke) that tell this parable follow it with texts that strongly hint at the answer. In Matthew the episode of Jesus' mother and brothers trying to speak with him follows the parable. That episode concludes with Jesus declaring that whoever does God's will is kin to him. In Luke the parable is immediately followed by a woman who cries out in blessing of Jesus' mother—to which Jesus responds, "Blessed rather are those who hear the word of God and obey it!" That which is to fill our lives is the doing of God's purposes. It is not enough simply to avoid what we think displeases God. Discipleship enacts faith by putting into practice what God would have us do.

That truth and this parable form an important balance to some caricatures of Lent. Lenten observances that focus only on what we will give up, especially when they are more in the nature of minor inconveniences than telling disciplines, miss the spirit of this season. Giving up may help us get our lives empty, swept, and put in order—but to leave it at that is to leave ourselves and our faith open to who knows what. Discipleship awaits our doing of the word, for in that action God's Spirit bears witness to God's presence in our lives and in all creation.

Holy God, dwell within me. Remove from me whatever stands in the way of relationship with you and others. Fill me with such grace and love as I will need to exercise grace and love in return. Amen.

SPIRITUAL EXERCISE

Make a list of habits, activities, and/or attitudes that you feel are not helpful in your following of Jesus. Alongside each one, record a more positive and faithful action, attitude, or habit that might take its place. Prayerfully determine how to begin making those exchanges. Seek God's help and strength and the support of others. Start with just one—and work gradually on the others.

THE GOD WHO PERSISTS

The Unjust Judge   *Luke 18:1-8*

Anna, our neighbor and friend, has shared meals with us and sat up on summer nights to count shooting stars (one hundred twenty-four one night in the middle of the Perseid showers in August). Anna, one of my mentors in faith, is also a widow.

So I listened with special interest several evenings ago when she told me about a Bible study she had led with a women's group based on the parable of the unjust judge. Several times in the conversation she brought up her dissatisfaction with it: "it" being not only the study but the parable. Her discomfort arose from one of the questions asked by the study guide: "How is the judge in the parable like God?" That did not sit well with Anna.

I confessed to her, as I do now to you, that I too have troubles with this parable. Persistence is truly a commendable virtue. Luke's preface of the parable about Jesus' telling it "about their need to pray always and not to lose heart" makes sense. But the parable and even its introduction also require great care in approach lest it take us down paths that generate more darkness than light.

Take the introduction. Luke intentionally connects the parable with the discipline of prayer. In doing so, however, we may presume the parable will provide illustration of both the human side and the divine side of prayer's equation. Prayer will be like one who persists and one who answers. Therefore, the widow will be expected to be like the petitioner in prayer and the judge be like God who hears our prayers and responds. Right? The danger of allegorizing parables, making every figure correspond to some higher meaning, comes to the forefront here.

We begin with a huge problem concerning the judge. Luke says nothing that would lead us to see God through this character. Quite the opposite. The parable opens with a twofold declaration that rules out any such connection. The judge "neither feared God nor had respect for people." The image speaks of an individual utterly self-contained: no need for God, no need for human community. When a widow comes to plead her case, he refuses her. The Hebrew Scriptures and oral traditions of Judaism leave no doubt about the obligation of judges to hear the causes of widows (and orphans). So this judge even turns his back on his own vocation and identity. And he would be the God-figure in the parable? I don't think so! Even when he relents and rules on her behalf, he does so for the wrong reason. He does not care about the justice of her case or the vulnerability of her person; he doesn't want to be bothered anymore. He doesn't want his reputation tarnished (the Greek word translated "wear out" literally means "to get a black eye").

So where or in whom do we encounter God in this parable? This story seems to be heavily weighted toward the human side of the prayer equation. Its traditional reading encourages our persistence in prayer. But at what point does persistence in prayer take the form of badgering and bothering? That is, after all, the language the parable uses to describe the woman's pleadings toward the judge. We might ask how the parable's counsel of persistence fits with Jesus' teachings on prayer in the Sermon on the Mount (Matthew 6:7-8). There we find a critique of prayer that presumes a hearing because of many words. The prayer Jesus counsels in that passage grows out of the trust that God already knows what we need before we ask. Persistence in that context becomes more of a disciplining of ourselves into awareness of our true needs than a breaking down of heaven's gates by relentless badgering.

But back to locating God in the parable; if anywhere, God takes form in this widow. It would not be the first time Jesus made such identification. The parable of the lost coin envisages God in a poor widow. And here: may we not perceive God in the persistence of this widow who continually comes seeking justice? After all, how many times and in how many ways has God persisted with us and all creation for the sake of justice? in hope of covenant? That is the nature and story of grace. God calls. We start forward, then fall back. God persists and does not give up. Grace does not let us go.

God's persistence is revealed in the tenacity of prophets who relentlessly call for justice when injustice reigns and equally insistent on grace when despair falls. The persistence of God is revealed in a Messiah who will not turn away from Jerusalem, come what may. God's persistence consistently takes the name and form of grace, especially in Lent. We taste grace in One who breaks bread with his betrayer. We receive grace in One who forgives crucifiers. We enter grace in One who restores his threefold denier by asking three times, "Do you love me?" Such persistence we meet in a widow who will not rest until right is restored. Such persistence we encounter in a God who will not let go of creation until it is restored.

> *God, I so easily let go of things and persons I need to hold on to. Teach me persistence by your grace that persists for the good of all creation. In Jesus Christ. Amen.*

SPIRITUAL EXERCISE

Consider God's persistent grace for you. Offer a prayer of thanks for such unrelenting love. Seek the Spirit's guidance in opening you to loving and doing justice more persistently.

Week 5

CUSTOMS AND CHOICES

*C*ustoms tend to proscribe our behavior. It is our custom here to do this or not do that. Customs provide a safety net of social necessity. And safety nets can be good when we find ourselves overwhelmed in times of crisis. They allow us to fall into step with the movement of others before us. We know what is expected of us without having to conjure expectations out of thin air. Customs are there for us, like it or not. This chapter's parables turn on customs related to suitable dress for weddings and what it means to be neighborly. We even briefly look at the customs of children at play.

But customs do not always fit the situation. How we have always done things may not be an adequate ethic for new situations. We need to make choices. Even if we fall back on doing things customarily, that is a choice. We could have done otherwise. These parables pose choices about the cost of proceeding one way or another and what we do with what has been entrusted to us.

Lent offers a season in which customs may play a large role in the educational and liturgical life of your church. Perhaps you have your own Lenten customs as you journey toward Jerusalem. There is nothing wrong with customs . . . so long as their routine does not become routine or their familiar territory lull you into complacency, so long as customs do not substitute for choice. Jesus kept the custom of the Passover, albeit in ways and with consequences altogether unexpected and uncustomary. Allow these parables to breathe new life into Lent's customs this year and fresh urgency into your choices of following the Messiah.

COUNTING THE COST

A Tower Builder and a King Going to War   *Luke 14:27-33*

When and where you hear a story can make a huge difference in how you hear it. I last preached on this text in a juvenile detention center located on the edge of the town where I live. The "camp" incarcerates teenagers for a variety of offenses: sex offenders, substance abusers, and the occasional manslaughter perpetrator.

So imagine yourself in the camp chapel in the shoes of one of those young women or men. You are serving a criminal sentence, convicted of an action that may have involved significant forethought or was just a spur of the moment decision. Either way, you have had your freedom stripped from you. You have paid a high price for the choice you made.

And then you hear the visiting chaplain read Luke 14:27-33. You may not know much about kings. You may have little acquaintance with building contractors. But you know from the inside what is at the core of those stories and the choices of those characters: the cost of actions.

When I spoke on this text, I asked the congregation that evening two questions: "If you had known what it would cost you, would you have still done what got you locked up here? And knowing now what it did cost, do you think you would repeat what you did?" I was then and still am under no illusions that those questions involve easy answers. Sometimes the costs of following or breaking the code of conduct on the streets appear—and maybe are—more severe than confinement by the state. I say that not to excuse what those young people had done and perhaps will do again. It is simply to recognize that the juvenile justice system is not the only one on the block that enforces costs on behavior.

When and where you hear a story can make a huge difference in how you hear it. You don't need to put yourself in another's shoes now. Consider where you are at this moment in your journey of faith and life. What costs do you need to consider to live as a disciple of Jesus in your family, church, community, and nation?

Sometimes those of us in the church and particularly in positions of leadership want to communicate that being a Christian comes without cost or difficulty. Indeed, if we believe some quarters of the church these days, being a Christian is the most direct and rapid way to success and prosperity—and I'm not just talking spiritually here! Check out the shelves of books that promise faith's material rewards, of naming and claiming it, of prayers whose bottom line involves getting ourselves right with God so God can do right by us. Years ago I recall a comic strip that "retold" the story of the rich young man who came to Jesus. After hearing the call to sell all he has and give to the poor, he begins to walk away. The "new revised" Jesus calls him to come back—just to say a prayer with him and accept him into his heart. "And don't worry," the comic-strip Jesus says, "about giving away stuff." The last frame of the strip shows the disciples with befuddled looks of *What happened there?*

The parables of the tower builder and the king who plans war bring us back to the Jesus of the Gospels, the Christ who reminds us that following has its costs. Actions do have consequences. Jesus tries to help us avoid being caught unawares of those consequences. Do what you must in order to carry through on the decision, or choose another way. It's not that Jesus here seeks to talk people out of following or to suggest that not following him is just as viable a spiritual path as following. Rather, Jesus would open eyes and spirits to the truth that discipleship is not a spiritual get-rich-quick scheme. It is the cross.

Discipleship carries the cross, which is literally what Jesus says in verse 27 to introduce these parables. Sometimes, but especially in Lent, we fall prey to considering minor indignities and inconveniences as a cross we bear. We may even make that connection to the seasonal detachments from chocolates or fats or whatever we give up for Lent. But notice that Jesus does not say in this introduction to the parables *a* cross but *the* cross. I take Jesus to mean that discipleship lives by a very different expression of power than what usually holds sway in the world at large. *The* cross asserts the extent of God's love. *The* cross proclaims Jesus' willingness to suffer violence rather than to do violence in the revealing of God's purposes and grace for this world. And in the case of discipleship, *the* cross reminds us that our following of Jesus does well to count the cost of loving with grace and serving with compassion. So to paraphrase the questions I asked of those youth:

- If you had known what discipleship would cost, would you still follow Jesus?

- And knowing now that discipleship carries the cross, will you still follow Jesus?

    God of mercy and love, grant me the strength to shoulder discipleship's load—and grant me the grace to know I do not do so alone. Amen.

Spiritual Exercise

Recall an occasion when faith "cost" you. What did that cost involve? What did that experience teach you? Consider a situation faced by you and/or your faith community that involves cost in the decision. Pray for the Spirit's guidance in weighing the cost and discerning what it may mean to carry the cross.

FOUNDATIONS

The Wise and Foolish Builders   *Matthew 7:24-27*

To satisfy the requirements for science credits in college, I took courses in geology. I did so for two reasons. One was a childhood curiosity about rocks and fossils. The other was a paranoia of chemistry and physics that high school classes validated. I do not remember many sessions in those geology courses, but one remains firmly planted in my mind.

It was the late 1960s. The craze of building homes on precarious view lots had become customary in many areas of the West Coast. Heavy rains had caused major mud slides in California, which swept away a number of expensive homes. For the entire class that day our geology professor fumed about the stupidity of building homes on unstable slopes in a region known for slides and earthquakes. He condemned the laxity of building codes that allowed construction where no secure foundation existed underneath. It was folly, and now others (as in "us") through insurance and disaster aid would bail out bad judgment on foundations.

Foundations make all the difference in the world. On that my professor and this parable of Jesus agree. The solid ones stand; the sandy ones fall. And great is their fall.

The biblical writers wrestle with the various foundations life offers. In the Hebrew Scriptures wisdom serves as a key to the basis upon which one builds a life: wisdom rooted in recognition of and faithfulness to God. In the New Testament, foundations for life are occasionally portrayed in the practical evidences our choices reveal. So, for example, Jesus can say, "Where your treasure is, there your heart will be also." Where we set our roots and lock our values, there we set our foundations. The worth of such foundations, as in the parable before us, will be assessed in their ability to help us weather whatever comes our way.

Life needs foundations that endure. We sometimes try to get by without such grounding in our lives. I do not just mean drifters out on the streets, people easy to single out and warn our children or grandchildren about becoming if they don't apply themselves. I also mean folks who read a new book or hear a new guru and become instant disciples—only to make a 180-degree turn when the next new idea or leader comes along. As long as things are fresh and exciting, the crowds will come. But responsible living requires lasting foundations. We need grounding that provides continuity when life's changing winds sometimes buffet us back and forth, threatening to uproot us. We need to choose our foundations wisely.

We have the option of building our whole lives upon persons, for whom the passage of time must bring eventual separation. Some parents have no lives outside their children. Husbands and wives may invest the total meaning of their existence in the other person and a sometimes idealized relationship. Such foundations can crumble when any one of a number of events transpires. A child chooses a career other than the one groomed for her by her parents. A spouse unexpectedly dies—or proves unfaithful in some regard. Most foundations, even those most beloved by us, have limitations.

In the biblical perspective God's presence in our lives provides the one sure foundation. Anchoring our lives in God, however, is not merely done in words that acknowledge such need. Setting our foundations in God comes in opening ourselves to God's working in and through us. Matthew's parable speaks clearly on just this point. We stand secure in our doing of the word of God's grace and love announced by Jesus. So do we find lasting foundations.

I enjoy exploring tidal pools on the coast. Clambering around huge boulders submerged only hours before, I often find at low tide many creatures clinging tightly to the rocks: masses of barnacles and mussels, clusters of starfish. The rocks are literally alive—and they literally give life. The relentless surf requires a solid mooring.

When life is easy and smooth, we may neglect our need for foundations that secure us. When our lives have no mooring or when we have settled for poor and shallow substitutes, we can easily be swept away by the surges of stress that wash over us. But if we fix ourselves in the presence of God, we will likely be surprised at what our lives can endure. Not because we are stronger than others, not because we are more experienced or more deserving or even more religious; but because our lives have tapped into deep foundations that will not fail us.

"The rain fell, the floods came, and the winds blew and beat on that house, but it did not fall." By the grace of God may our lives find such firm and lasting foundations in Jesus Christ.

Reveal to me, O God, where I may sink my life's foundation securely in your presence, deeply in your love. In Jesus Christ. Amen.

Spiritual Exercise

Read aloud Matthew 7:24-27. Call to mind experiences where you found your life and/or faith buffeted about. To what and on whom did you cling for support? What did you learn about foundations in those times and since? Consider actions or disciplines you might take up in this season of Lent to secure your foundations in Christ. Pray for help in that mooring of your life in God.

WHICH ONE OF YOU?

A Friend Asks for Help at Night   *Luke 11:5-8*

Be honest. Having read this parable, does it leave you with questions? It should. Verses 5-7 in Greek are one long question strung together. "'Suppose one of you has a friend,'" elsewhere translated as "'which one of you has a friend,'" aims the parable's question at the outset squarely toward the reader or listener. Who is this "friend" the parable wants us to consider? Is it the friend who comes knocking at midnight, or is it the friend whose sleep is disturbed by the late-night commotion at his door? The distinction makes a difference, and the text leaves it unclear which is intended. Depending on our perspective of the friend, we may hear this parable as an encouragement to pray with persistence (the Greek word more accurately means "shamelessness"). Or it may lead us to hear this parable assuring trust of how much more God will hear our prayers out of grace as opposed to one who is shamed into action.

Stepping back into the original context of this parable's speaking may help us hear Jesus' story anew in the light of Lent. The parable's most important dynamic is village life in first-century Judea. Hospitality toward friend or stranger weighed heavily on the obligation to receive those who came to you. Akin to current Middle Eastern cultures, village life involved a shame and honor culture. To neglect obligations like hospitality resulted in shame, not simply in the judgment of the one left unattended but in the sight of the entire community. The concern not to be shamed is all about reputation. On the other hand, one who could be trusted to keep such obligations as friend and host would be honored. In the parable the friend who eventually responds does so not out of friendship but seemingly so as not to be shamed.

Luke has set this parable in the midst of teachings on prayer, preceded by his version of the Lord's Prayer and followed by assurances of God's hearing of us. Given that context, it is difficult *not* to hear this parable as anything but an assurance of a "how much more" will God hear us than one who acts only in response to avoid shame. And since Luke alone records this parable, that contextual setting in prayer looms large in our hearing and interpretation.

So how does this translate into our daily practice of discipleship and our attending to this parable in the midst of Lent? Let us return to that open question of which friend this parable invites us to consider and learn from.

The one who comes calling at night does so out of necessity. Hospitality to the one who has presented himself as a guest requires that a meal be provided. This individual could not act otherwise, at least honorably, given the obligations of hospitality in that community. So this parable is *not* about pestering God in prayer with optional frills that would make our lives "nicer" or more comfortable. The story seen through the lens of this friend urges us to bring to God the pressing matters of our existence. Indeed, it urges us to prayer that provides for the need of neighbor. For whom is this gift of bread? Not for the friend but for the one who has come as guest. The prayer is for the *other*. To return to Luke's context, Jesus had taught his disciples to pray for God's provision of *our* daily bread. Notice the pronoun. Not me. At least, not *just* me. "Give *us* each day *our* daily bread" (emphasis added). Then follows this parable where the providing of another's bread brings one friend to another. Sometimes the answer to another's daily bread comes in what God in Christ may provide through us—if we are open and hospitable. If we are faithful.

But remember, the parable also makes it possible to view as the friend in question the one whose sleep is disturbed. "Which one of you" would respond as did he with "don't bother me; the door is locked; the kids are in bed." In the culture of that day, the question of "which one" would be answered by "no one!" No one would answer like that. Not unless you would be shamed.

Then again, if the truth be told, "which one of you" could also be answered, "every one." Who among us has not declined to help another human being? Who among us has not turned a deaf ear to what we did not want to hear because the timing was wrong? Did not Jesus also tell a story of a priest and Levite walking by a wounded man on the Jericho road? Did not Jesus tell a story of children sitting in the marketplace in order to indict those who did not want to hear what John—and then he—had to say because it was out of step?

"Which one of you has a friend" also asks a question related to the unfolding story of Jesus' passion. For when it came to the practice of hospitality, how did folks welcome the guest Jesus? A friend like Peter denied. A friend like Judas betrayed. A neighbor like Caiaphas turned a deaf ear to truth. A neighbor like Pilate vainly washed his hands of an execution that he ordered. And one who came seeking to give himself as bread had no one come Friday to offer a crumb of welcome.

In Lent the parable's question moves from "which one of you has a friend": to "which one of you will be a friend" to those cast out and condemned, to those who rely on our words and our commitments, to the One who in saving you would save all.

God, you hear us with grace and respond in love. May our lives practice such conversation with others. For your sake and in your example. In Jesus Christ. Amen.

SPIRITUAL EXERCISE

Think of a friend who has provided for you, perhaps at great cost. Pray to be such a friend for another, even a stranger.

Games and Wisdom

Children in the Marketplace   *Matthew 11:16-19*

It is no coincidence that a parable Jesus tells about children playing games ends up in this chapter on customs. Games give children a playful introduction to adult ways of doing things. Do you want to form cultures as well as habits? Don't talk to a child about socialization. Play a game! After all, games require rules. And what are customs and traditions but rules we have devised for how we will live in a particular place as a particular people. Do you want to anger a child in a game? Don't play by the rules! Peek during hide and seek. Count to twenty instead of one hundred. Or in the context of this parable from Matthew, don't dance when you're supposed to dance. Don't play sad when it's time to play sad.

Jesus is not grinding an ax here about children or taking them to task for playing when they should be doing other things, like acting more grown up. This is the same Jesus who told some adult followers they could learn about the sovereign realm of God from the attitude of a child. For all we know, when Jesus uttered those particular words, the child he set in their midst as an example may have been playing on the floor while he spoke.

No, Jesus in this parable seems more focused on the function of play as socialization. The games children play merely mimic how institutions and communities set up the rules and insist that individuals (adults) conform to expectations. Sometimes you can dance; sometimes you can cry—but don't get those times in the game mixed up. Because life, like games, is all about fitting in and going with the flow. Childhood games prepare adult lives to place a premium on conformity. Play by the rules or get out. Color inside the lines. Do as you're told.

Customs and traditions can play positive roles in shaping our life, but at times they err on the side of confinement. They can be quite unforgiving of those who are perceived, rightly or wrongly, to march to the beat of a different drummer.

Jesus minces no words in terms of his intent in this parable. John and now Jesus have been the victims of arbitrary rules of institutional games. John caught flack for his austerity. Jesus gets criticized for eating with the wrong kinds of folks. It's not just that you can't please all the people all the time; sometimes you can't please anyone. Here Jesus and John go condemned by the same people for opposing behaviors. So Jesus takes their "game-playing" to task, knowing full well his critics fast like John and feast like Jesus. The problem is that both John and Jesus are out of step with established norms. Both of their ministries have disturbed the powers that be, politically and religiously. And now for John, and soon for Jesus, not playing by the community's rules will be costly.

The Lenten undercurrent in this parable is clear and ominous. The preceding text told of John's arrest and imprisonment, a situation that will eventuate in his execution. In the next chapter a sabbath healing by Jesus will launch a conspiracy whose aim is "how to destroy him" (Matt. 12:14). Games can become deadly serious.

So where is the good news in this parable? Ironically, hope resides in other "children." Both Matthew and Luke narrate this parable. The versions closely parallel one another except for their endings. In Matthew: "wisdom is vindicated by her deeds." In Luke: "wisdom is vindicated by all her children." There are other children related to this parable besides those who catcall for not conforming to the rules of their games. These others would be the children who do not demonize John or castigate Jesus. These would be the ones who attend to the new words and ways of John and Jesus. These children understand that God's reign ushers in a new set of times for us to live and assess what is right and fitting. The game has changed.

Such is the wisdom this parable offers. In the Hebrew faith of Jesus, wisdom was not synonymous with intellect. Rather, wisdom had to do with how we conduct our lives in practical ways, given our knowledge and experience of God. Wisdom is not what we know about God but how we live in response to God. The wisdom sought in this parable back then was the recognition that new times had come in the persons and ministries of John and Jesus. The wisdom sought in this parable now is the realization that we still live in those new times. This parable's wisdom concerning God's realm invites consideration that playing out of sync with conforming powers and traditions may still be the way of faith. For we would be the children of God's wisdom, not the world's. Christ beckons us to play by the wise rules of grace and Spirit.

> *Teach me to play anew, O God. Set me free to dance when your grace brings joy. Open me to grieve when such times come. And allow me always to live aware and responsive to you. Amen.*

SPIRITUAL EXERCISE

Make a list of the games you most remember from childhood. Think of what you learned in the playing of those games about yourself, about community, about ways to live. Reread Matthew 11:16-19. When have you felt out of sync from those around you? In what ways did those experiences relate to your convictions or your faith? Pray for God's leading to live as a child of God, even and especially when that seems out of step with those around you.

FUTURE RISK

The Talents   *Matthew 25:14-30*

I naturally tend to play things safe. Maybe it is my Midwest upbringing, where "better safe than sorry" has long guided young and not-so-young minds. Maybe it is the DNA strings of my genetic coding.

So when I hear the parable of the talents read in church, a part of me would like to raise my hand and say, "Excuse me, pastor, but can I speak on behalf of that third servant? You know, the one who went out and buried the talent in the field. Do you mean to say he was wrong? Why, last week at the trustees meeting, I thought we all decided it would be a good thing not to touch those reserve savings, save them for a rainy day. Or what about the time the council thought it best not to take a chance on funding that new program for the homeless? 'We can't risk what we're doing now for something we don't know is going to work.' Isn't that what we said? So how on earth can we smile and nod our heads in condemnation of this poor fellow who pretty much did the same thing we did?"

Parables are risky. We think Jesus is talking about those other folks over there back then; and all of a sudden the words catch us where we live and put us in the middle of the action . . . or inaction. Even when we've heard these stories over and over—and this parable has a way of popping up most every year at stewardship time—something catches us off guard. For me that something is the third servant. In my heart I find it hard to fault this individual. He sees someone who won't take a loss of property well, so he does the safest thing possible. He avoids risk and buries the talent.

Now here is where language can create a problem for interpretation. Bury a talent? Well, no wonder this person is condemned! You can't hide your gift, whether it's playing the piano or teaching a child or advocating for the vulnerable. You've got to use what God has blessed you with in life. Use those talents!

But let's step back into the parable's day and language. "Talent" was neither a skill nor a God-given ability. "Talent" was a particular sum of money—in fact, a whopping sum of money. As noted in the reading on the unforgiving servant (chapter 4), one talent equaled six thousand denarii. A denarius was the average wage for a worker in that time. So let us remember: this servant was being entrusted with the equivalent of 16.44 years of wages—and that's without a single day off. Multiply that number times the figure you report on your IRS Form 1040 as annual income. You are entrusted with a check for that multiplied amount by someone you judge to be a harsh man whom you fear. So will you go out and do everything you can to risk what, given a five-day work week, would have taken you well over twenty years to earn on your own? Or will you play it safe and make your return no less than what he gave?

Many stewardship sermons notwithstanding, this parable invites us to an experience far more profound than whether we will sing in the choir this year or what amount we will write on our pledge form. This parable about using what has been entrusted to us goes far beyond that. "Talents" in its original meaning pushes us to recognize that something much larger is at stake here.

That something is the future and what we willingly risk for the sake of future we say belongs to God. In light of this parable we must first risk our infatuation with fear. Fear, that great motivator of human behavior, drives the third servant's actions: "I knew that you were a harsh man . . . ; so I was afraid." But fear is a motive driven by and leading to death: death of relationship, of hope, of consciousness. Fear can motivate through its threat of eliminating the future. But as the parable reveals, fear is inadequate for life lived in the face of God's realm. Fear only works on the basis of death.

God's realm has to do with life. God's realm relates to the eventual undoing of death. Once we remove fear as a motive, we can risk for the sake of the future. That is the thrust of Jesus' life and passion. Fear of what may happen in Jerusalem does not deter Jesus' present journey. Rather, trust in what God will bring to pass enables Jesus to risk the Jerusalem path. There the parable and Lent converge. Our trust in God's realm, present and eventual, encourages us to let loose of fear. How better can we offer what we have been given and become the persons God has gifted us to be than by choosing to live not by the threat of fear but in the promise of hope?

So do not be afraid. The future is not only worth the risk; the future comes in risk!

God, help me to know you, not in harshness to be feared but in graciousness to be trusted. And in such trust move me to act for the sake of your future. In Jesus Christ. Amen.

Spiritual Exercise

Consider what role(s) fear plays in your actions and inactions. Reread the parable as if written to address your fear. What is fear keeping you from discovering about God, about the future, about yourself? Pray for wisdom and courage in risking to live as one entrusted with the gift of trust and the promise of future.

UPSIDE DOWN, INSIDE OUT

I enjoy the stories of O. Henry, with their last-second twists and ironic turns. But O. Henry had nothing on Jesus. The rabbi overturns pious presumptions and societal customs with words and actions that come at us out of the blue.

We have already encountered Jesus' appetite for lacing his parables with the unexpected: a mustard seed's lavish shelter, the forgiveness of outlandish debt repaid with unthinkable violence. But in this chapter's parables, topsy-turvy becomes the norm. The oxymoron of a good Samaritan takes its place with a maddeningly (or is it offensively?) gracious employer. A father prematurely divides inheritance (but not love) between two sons until we wonder just who is the prodigal in this story. Then comes the parable of the great judgment. There the sacrament of encounter with Christ occurs not in sanctuary and ritual but in community with the least and least likely among us.

These parables speak of how God's reign turns this world's orders inside out and upside down. Such reversal goes to the heart of Lent. The way to Jerusalem does not follow the path of least resistance. The way to Jerusalem does not tell a tale of one who makes it possible for me to shoot the winning basket or succeed in business or war by crushing my competitors. The way to Jerusalem reveals the calling to meet hatred with love, to speak truth in the face of lies, and to forgive one's enemies. Lent prepares us for discipleship that cuts against the grain of the powers that be, in trust and in hope of the Power who will be, world without end. Amen.

NEIGHBORS AND FENCES

The Good Samaritan   *Luke 10:25-37*

"Good fences make good neighbors," asserts Robert Frost's poem "Mending Wall." Those words have traveled with me for some time. Even so, I don't believe I read the whole poem until just a few years ago. As a result, I long assumed that Frost simply celebrated this folk wisdom about fences. I figured the poem to be an ode to white picket fences in villages or serpentine rock walls in the country, defining boundaries and maintaining the privilege of privacy.

After all, one need not be a New England farmer to see the value in fences. My mind still carries the view from the backyard of my childhood home in St. Louis. Looking north or south, in the corridor between rows of homes on one side and a grass alley on the other, an endless series of fences enclosed every backyard for as far as I could see. The newer Cyclone fence of the Plochers, the older wire fence of Mrs. Sewell: I grew up in a neighborhood defined by fences. I suspect we all did in one way or another.

I came to discover other fences that defined our neighborhood. I played a lot with the Timm boys, older than me but from a good Lutheran family. Jackie M. was my age and lived no farther than the Timms, but we hardly ever played. I recall asking him over for lunch one day, and he came. But never again—and I was asked to break bread (with peanut butter) at his house only once. Jackie came from a good Catholic family. It took me a while to realize that somebody had put a fence between us that wasn't as easily climbed as those between the houses. In those days identities of Protestant and Catholic ran deeper than categories checked off on a census form. Those identities fenced you in, and others out.

"Good fences make good neighbors." Good fences kept the neighbors' dogs from trampling your garden. Good fences kept young kids from running amuck among other people's barbecues.

Good fences, of a different sort, sought to insure we didn't end up with African American neighbors, not to mention in-laws. Whether the fence came constructed of steel or attitude: good fences made good neighbors by reminding us of who belonged where, with "good" defined by acting accordingly.

"Good fences make good neighbors." That attitude predates my 1950s St. Louis neighborhood by at least two millennia. A lawyer asks Jesus a question about fences. He doesn't use the word *fence* per se, but it's there. Having come to test Jesus and then finding himself questioned by Jesus, the lawyer seeks to pin Jesus down: "Who is my neighbor?" The question traces back to the lawyer's own understanding of what the law requires to inherit eternal life. "You shall love the Lord your God . . . [you shall love] your neighbor as yourself." Loving God is relatively clear. But if love of neighbor is involved, then who is my neighbor? What are the limits? Where is the fence that separates neighbor from stranger or enemy or whomever the obligation to love omits?

In answer, Jesus doesn't point at the crowd and say, "There's a neighbor" or "There's *not* one." Jesus tells a story. A man on the road between Jerusalem and Jericho is robbed, beaten, and left for dead. This road is notorious for such events. It follows a steep canyon, dropping in seventeen or so miles from twenty-five hundred feet above sea level to eight hundred feet below sea level. Marked with high ridges, secluded caves, and blind corners, it offers ideal settings for ambush.

That potential for being waylaid probably played into the decisions of the priest and Levite not to stop. Delays on that road only increased exposure to danger. And who is to say that what looks like a beaten traveler is not a robber in disguise, with cohorts ready to victimize any who take the bait? Besides, the priest and Levite have religious considerations. If they are on their way to serve at the Temple, stopping poses another danger. Leviticus 21 forbids priests to touch a corpse. To do otherwise makes one ritually unclean, unable to perform sacred duties. The priest and Levite are not monsters but persons with responsibilities who have to choose among competing duties: to a known Temple or an unknown stranger.

In a sense, established religious tradition built a fence that argued against these two from risking aid. So the parable moves outside that tradition to lift up the exemplar of neighbor. "But a Samaritan while traveling came near him; and when he saw him, he was moved with pity." For hundreds of years Samaritans and Jews lived in hatred. To the Jews Samaritan religion represented a heretical mingling of Judaism and local customs. Samaritans promoted their own temple on Mount Gerizim as rival to Jerusalem. When it came to Jews and Samaritans, it wasn't just that good fences made good neighbors; you needed good fences to keep out bad neighbors.

Jesus' parable demolishes that ancient fence, not by denying past history and old stories but by redefining neighbor. "Which of these three was a neighbor to the man who fell into the hands of the robbers?" "*The one who showed him mercy*" (emphasis added). "Go and do likewise."

Fences do not make good neighbors; good neighbors transcend fences. As long as the lawyer could draw distinctions between those who were neighbor and those who were not, he could place limits on the obligation to love. But where the lawyer sought a fence line to define who qualifies for love and who does not, Jesus got out a pair of wire cutters. Neighbor resides not in pedigree, residency, or proximity: neighbor takes shape in need and opportunity to aid.

I wonder how well we practice such neighborliness in our churches, not to mention our wider communities. It is far easier to be in the fencing business. In the days of the civil rights movement, it was said that the most segregated hour in the United States was 11:00 AM Sunday. Some suggest it still is. And not just racially either. Liberal versus conservative, clergy versus laity, old versus young, local congregation versus district or conference leadership, evangelical versus ecumenical, gay versus straight. We have this innate ability to dwell on things that differentiate us and then build walls to insure we keep our side pure. We erect our fences to keep it so . . . by keeping *us* so. But when it comes to God's mercy, fences are made for trespassing. What else can be said when Jesus trots out a Samaritan to exemplify neighborliness?

Even that poem of Robert Frost, which I long assumed to celebrate the need of fences, does just the opposite. At both its opening and near its close, Frost asserts: "Something there is that doesn't love a wall." That something in the parable is the mercy of God, revealed in the neighborliness of a Samaritan. A mercy that makes shambles of any would-be fences between us and neighbor, a mercy that incarnates life eternal by embodying love eternal. May we go and do likewise.

> *Break down the fences, O God, that separate me from neighbor.*
> *In keeping me from others, those bounds keep me from you.*
> *Amen.*

Spiritual Exercise

On one side of a paper or journal page, list "fences" that divide individuals and groups in your church, community, and/or nation. On the other side identify the fences you help to maintain. Focus on one of those dividing walls in light of this parable. Seek the Spirit's guidance in what Jesus' words of "go and do likewise" may mean for you and this fence.

THE PROBLEM WITH GRACE

The Gracious Employer   *Matthew 20:1-16*

I know, I know. We love to sing of grace as amazing and sweet-sounding. But sometimes grace grates on our ears and spirits. Because for grace to be grace, it has to be free, unearned. And *unearned* is not a good word in the lexicon of our society. People need to work for what they get. People need to earn their keep. Otherwise, what kind of a world would we live in?

Well, Jesus says, there's this owner of a vineyard who goes out and hires people to work in his fields. He pays people who worked one hour in the cool of evening the same amount as he pays those who worked and sweated through a full day out in the heat and sun. Where is the justice in that, we ask? Where is the shop steward handing out picket signs, calling the owner to task for unfair practices? Where are the other vineyard owners meeting in closed session, demanding of their errant colleague "a fair day's wage only for a fair day's work." Where are the church administrators cautioning against such an irresponsible suggestion? After all, listen to Jesus here and folks might think that their labors above and beyond the call of duty go unappreciated (we're too polite to come right out and say "unrewarded") by a God who eventually gives everybody the same when all is said and done.

What kind of a world is this parable about? "The kingdom of heaven is like . . ." The kingdom or sovereign realm of God is all about the problem of *grace*. Now maybe we could convene a group of scholars to deny the authenticity of this word as attributable to Jesus and thus get ourselves off a very sticky question. However, this parable does not stand in isolation as the only instance where grace seems to contradict what is fair and just. It is there from the beginning. Literally "in the beginning," the opening words to the book of Genesis.

Piercing through the cracks of even those foundation stories of our faith are instances of a troubling sort of grace. Cain slays his brother, his own flesh and blood. He deserves to die. Not only does Cain live, but God promises to act in vengeance against anyone who kills Cain. The grace of God protects the criminal. Where is the justice in that?

The offense of such grace takes another ironic embodiment on the hill of Golgotha, where Jesus dies crucified between two thieves. While the Gospels insist on Jesus' innocence, they make no such claims about the thieves. One of those thieves even confesses that he deserves such a fate, an extreme statement given the nature of crucifixion. Yet that thief also asks Jesus to remember him in his kingdom. What happens next might seem anything but just to decent folk who struggle day in and day out to live good lives. "'Today you will be with me in Paradise.'" Grace embraces a condemned man, one whose recent past and perhaps much longer has merited such condemnation. Is it just that such a person receives grace for a mere deathbed confession? The words of the parable might voice the feelings of some about this last-minute gift. "'These last worked only one hour, and you have made them equal to us.'" Grace can offend.

Such grace comes to the fore in the meaning of Jesus' cross. Had God chosen to act and deal with creation solely on the basis of justice, there would have been no need for a cross. Just broadcast the rules, lay out the game plan, and let our actions speak for themselves. However, the grace of God exposed that—instead of letting our actions speak for themselves and the chips fall where they may—God chose to act on our behalf. In that cruciform action, God reveals that our justification in God's eyes is not how morally or piously we conduct our life and affairs. Acceptance hinges on how broadly and lovingly God's grace welcomes all. A grace for which all that I do and say are, at best, its effects—never its cause.

Part of the time such grace is no problem for us. We cherish the free and loving acceptance of us that it assures. The problem of grace tends to come when others enter the picture. Sometimes we prefer that God deal with us according to grace but with others according to what they deserve.

The parable illustrates that part of the problem with grace. In spite of knowing the amount they had agreed to work for, the original workers resent what the later workers receive. So they confront their employer. Do they have a point? Absolutely. But it is not the point of this parable, which is the grace of the owner . . . and through his character, the grace of God. A grace that supercedes justice. A grace that seeks the same gift, the same life for all.

"'Am I not allowed to do what I choose with what belongs to me? Or are you envious because I am generous?'"

That is the problem with God's grace . . . and that problem is our salvation.

Turn me, O God, from resenting the grace you extend to others.
May I celebrate its gift to my foes and friends alike. Amen.

SPIRITUAL EXERCISE

In your journal reflect on your own experiences of grace extended to and by you. Note any problems you have had with grace, either in accepting God's love for your life or accepting God's love for those you find undeserving. Read over what you have written. Pray over what you have written. Listen in those words and prayer for ways in which grace may turn and shape you.

PRODIGALS

The Lost Son and the Father's Love   Luke 15:11-24

Neither Jesus nor Luke use the word *prodigal* in telling or recording this parable. It is a label the church only later superimposed upon it. And with great success. Say aloud "prodigal son" in a congregation, and you will likely see heads nod in recognition and familiarity. "Oh, yes, the prodigal. My cousin's nephew was such a boy. Wandered off. Got himself good and lost doing you know what with you know who. Made a mess of his life. But just like the story, he came to his senses and returned home. Got his act together. Made amends. And now that prodigal is part of the family again. Thank God!"

There is nothing wrong with that story, that joy, that thanksgiving. Would that all those whose faces and memories come to mind with the mention of "prodigal" turn out that way. But that's not the whole story of this parable. Lo and behold, there's more than one prodigal here! I should tell you up front that we don't get to the elder son until the next reading—so that's not the other prodigal I mean. The other prodigal is the father.

Prodigal: "recklessly wasteful . . . profuse in giving . . . a person given to luxury or extravagance" (*The American Heritage Dictionary*). The church imposed "prodigal" on this parable out of that first understanding of its definition. The younger child took all he had and "squandered his property in dissolute living." But sometimes the church acts just like the first disciples and misunderstands Jesus. We want to talk about seats in glory and positions of privilege, when Jesus wants to move the conversation to service and humility. We want to pull out our swords and hack away at the opponents, when Jesus knows violence begets violence . . . and love eventually begets love. We want to tell everybody about a prodigal son, when Jesus wants to tell us about a prodigal parent.

"Profuse in giving." This parent divides up the shares of the family property, an act usually reserved until after death. For the younger boy, his dad can't die soon enough; and the father goes along with it. Is giving profusely a good way to teach responsibility?

"A person given to extravagance." The boy is walking back home, destitute, a failure. He has his speech of remorse duly memorized and rehearsed. Nothing in the text suggests any insincerity on his part. Now is an ideal time for this young man to learn a hard lesson about humility. And who else should be in charge of hard lessons but a parent? How else can we make sure our children understand the gravity of their mistakes? How else can we restore the authority that belongs to this relationship? The boy has acted as though the father couldn't die quick enough. So now we stand alongside that father as he waits and watches the youthful prodigal slowly walk toward the house and kin once abandoned. We would understand the father if a gate swings closed or a door locks tight. We might even understand if the father receives the wanderer only after listening to every heart-wrenching word.

But how can we understand the extravagance of this old prodigal? What do we make of someone who acts as though the apology is secondary to the return, who runs to meet the one who should be crawling through the mud for what has been done? Years ago I heard Kenneth Bailey speak of this parable's affront. Even more shameful than what the son has done is how the father now caves in. Such an act undermines authority, not just in family but in community. For if such a one returns home and receives such honor and extravagant welcome, what will that mean for the village, for the society?

In Dr. Bailey's estimation such an act in that time merited punishment—not of the son, mind you, but of the father. The parable runs deeper than just a story of family reunion. Recall the complaint against Jesus that Luke identifies at the beginning of this chapter: "'This fellow welcomes sinners and eats with them.'" This parable arises out of conflict in that community over respectability and community standards. Jesus has gone outside those bounds. In the narrative, and subtly within the parable, we are on the way to Jerusalem. At stake is what will be done with one whose love and grace is prodigal.

We are not done with this parable, for another character stands on its edges. This portion closes by asserting that the dead live and the lost are found. The order of those statements implies that death and life may not be as consequential as whether one is lost or found. The movement between death and life, lost and found occurs in the parable through a prodigal's love for a prodigal. The movement between death and life, lost and found occurs in our lives by the prodigal love incarnate for us in Jesus' ministry and passion.

> *You find and enliven me with such extravagant grace, O God: given in creation, affirmed in redemption, promised in hope. Help me remember I am a child and heir of such prodigal love. Amen.*

SPIRITUAL EXERCISE

Remember times when you may have had cause to approach God as did this younger son. As you remember those times, imagine the scene of this parable's welcome of the one returning. God has welcomed you. God has graced you. Even before you start "home," God's arms open wide in embrace. Consider how God's embrace of you invites your welcome of others.

THE CHILDREN OF GOD

A Father's Love of a Dutiful Child   *Luke 15:25-32*

Have you heard the story of the introductory bus tour to heaven? On arriving, people board one of those luxury coaches with windows that stretch from floor to ceiling. The driver provides a running narrative while taking the passengers around the precincts of Paradise. It becomes clear that folks tend to cluster in neighborhoods based on religious affiliation. So the driver points out when driving through the Anglican neighborhood, then the Church of God in Christ suburb, and so forth. The noise on the bus is a bit loud, as folks are quite happy to find out they have arrived in the state of eternal bliss. And the neighborhood people don't seem to mind all the shouting and singing coming from inside the bus. But then the bus slows, and the driver calls the passengers to order. "There'll be no noise for the next five minutes." The bus grows silent. Reflective coverings on the window drop down, the kind where you can see out from the inside but not see in from the outside. The bus passes through a gate enclosed by high walls. The neighborhood within seems no different. Finally, the bus exits another gate, and looking back it is clear that the neighborhood is walled around completely. The driver signals the OK to talk again.

"Say driver, what's the deal with that place? Why couldn't we make any noise?"

"Well, that's where those folks from the United Church of Christ live. They think they're the only ones who made it here, and God doesn't want them to get upset."

(Author's note: I belong to the United Church of Christ. Feel free to substitute your own group in the punch line.)

Humor and scripture may be an oxymoron for some. Religion is serious. Faith is no laughing matter. But I cannot help but picture the closing scene of this parable with the father's face breaking into a smile. Not a smirk, mind you. He has not come out of the house to rub the younger's return and welcome in the elder's face. I do not even see that smile as one of those self-assured, "Oh, you'd think this was funny if you were smart enough to get it."

No, the father has emerged from a celebration where everything is smiles and laughter. A lost son, a dead son, has showed up. How can you not smile at the experience of such restoration? How can you not carry such joy out of that room wherever you go? Even when the father leaves the room to face the elder son who lashes out with resentment, the fact is that the elder too is this parent's child. That one also remains loved.

I see a smile written across this parent's reply to the elder's anger. The NRSV drops the ball on the father's first word in verse 31. It is not *son*, a word weighted with implications of "heir"—the cause of the younger's initial misstep and now the elder's jealousy. The Greek word translates better as "child," a word of endearment. The father had earlier raced out before any word of remorse or repentance was spoken in order to embrace the younger with the tender acceptance of his child. Now, he goes out of the house to embrace his other child. Any misgivings about heir and inheritance are quickly settled: "'all that is mine is yours.'" This parent, this love, acts to banish all barriers to the essential relationship that is theirs as parent and child. In doing so, this parent, this love, acts to banish all barriers to the essential relationship between elder and younger as brothers. In bitterness the elder spews out against "'this son of yours.'" In tenderness the father seeks to share the joyous return of "'this brother of yours.'" You cannot say such words with a frown or a scowl of disapproval.

Do not misunderstand. This serious parable has serious consequences. If the opening three verses of chapter 15 are accurate, this story has been told to those who might have been quite at home in the shoes and fears of the elder brother. Like him, they despised choices made by Jesus about table fellowship. Like him, they worked long and hard and never disobeyed. The Pharisees and scribes are not irreligious people. On the contrary, they resolve to do everything they possibly can to keep the Torah. Some even describe the minutiae of oral traditions that have accumulated as a "fence" around the Torah, to prevent its accidental transgression.

By keeping those opening verses to chapter 15 in context with the parables that follow, Luke leaves the door open for linking the Pharisees and scribes with the elder brother. To some that amounts to an explicit condemnation of the scribes and Pharisees. But is it? Remember the words spoken by the father to the elder: "Son, you are always with me and all that is mine is yours." These are not words of estrangement but of relationship. These are not words of schism but of reconciliation. These are not words intended to condemn but to preserve.

The parable leaves the ending open. We do not know what the elder will do. Then again, we don't know but that the younger will leave home and squander it all again. The parable doesn't tell us. The parable does tell us how much this parent loves these two children, doing so at great risk to reputation in the community and in relationship with those offspring. The father refuses to choose between the boys. This parent will love both, come what may.

We are so used to this parable's surprising welcome of the prodigal child that we may miss the equally stunning surprise of its acceptance of the dutiful child. Perhaps like our opening story, we are so prepared for heaven to be populated with all our prodigal friends that it may take us aback when we discover the stuffy self-righteous folk who find a home in God's grace as well. Whose presence will surprise us the most? Who will be surprised by God's calling us "child"? We don't have to wait for the bus tour to discover that surprise. It begins now in a grace that embraces all God's children. Let those who have ears to hear and eyes to see—smile!

You call me your child, O God. You receive me in love, even before I reciprocate your love. You are with me always, even

*when I would shut you out. You call me your child and so name
me with love. Amen.*

SPIRITUAL EXERCISE

Whom do you have the greatest difficulty accepting? Who has the
greatest difficulty accepting you? Envision yourselves in the presence of God. God speaks the same word to you both: *child.* What
will you do about that?

Meeting Jesus

The Great Judgment   *Matthew 25:31-46*

"Meeting Jesus." For some, the phrase serves as a euphemism for any serious decision. In one documentary of the 1992 presidential campaign, a scene depicts a campaign leader calling for several key persons to be brought in because it's time for them to meet Jesus. The time for debate and discussion has ended. The time for decision making and action taking has come.

It's time to meet Jesus.

This book has not quite ended. After this reading, there remains an epilogue to walk with you through the final days of Holy Week into Easter. I hope you have been encountering Jesus in the parables and reflections read to date and that they have made your journey through Lent one of renewal and insight. But of all the parables Jesus told, this one stands unique. While the language of metaphor remains, the core of this parable speaks a distinctly personal and direct word about where—and in whom—we encounter Jesus. It's time to meet Jesus.

I was hungry and you gave me food,
I was thirsty and you gave me something to drink,
I was a stranger and you welcomed me,
I was naked and you gave me clothing,
I was sick and you took care of me,
I was in prison and you visited me.

Just as you did it to one of the least of these who are members of my family, you did it to me.

The church never has gotten over the shock of these words. The parable doesn't bless the faith of those who knew all along they ministered to Jesus by taking care of others. They flat out didn't know. Looking back across the landscape of their lives, those whom the parable calls righteous have no remembrance of a needy Jesus.

"When was it that we saw *you?*" (emphasis added) they ask, not once, not twice, but three times. Perhaps the king has made a mistake and confused them with others. Perhaps they are not blessed at all. They have no knowledge of ever having done such things for Jesus. At least they never thought they did.

The blessed didn't recognize the glimmer of Jesus' eye in the hollowed-out gaze of an addict or the gaunt face of a bereaved parent and therefore treated that person differently. They simply cared for these folks because, well, who knows why. The parable doesn't specify their reasons. It certainly doesn't say they did it because faith demanded it of them. The parable just says they are shocked to hear they'd cared for Jesus all this time.

Likewise, surprise and shock describe the reaction of the remaining people in this parable. They too are reduced to asking when it was they saw Jesus in need and didn't take care of him. They receive the same answer, though cast now in the negative: "'Just as you did not do it to one of the least of these, you did not do it to me.'"

Jesus does not condemn these folks for *not* recognizing him. Because if the truth be told, *nobody* in this parable saw Jesus in need. But at the least, or should I say *in* the least, those blessed of God saw needy human beings and responded by serving. They may not have seen Christ, but they saw the homeless or the bereaved or the AIDS victim. They saw the one turned out and turned away because of a differing sexual orientation. They saw the undocumented alien or the felon or the Arab-American or whoever is encountered with ache of body or emptiness of spirit or as an outcast from community. And in seeing them, they serve Christ. In seeing them, they meet Jesus.

The parable doesn't come right out and say it, but one wonders if the second group ever did see these people in need. Maybe they did with their eyes, the way you get used to driving by poverty on a city street without another thought. But it takes discipline to keep the optic nerve connected to the heart, the will, and whatever else produces human compassion. If you don't see the needs of others in such a way that they get inside of you, it's easy to walk away. To turn the head. To click the channel from news on how many thousands of refugees poise on the edge of starvation back to the reality shows that have nothing to do with reality. If you listen carefully, those accursed in this parable are not accused of doing anything wrong. Simply, yet profoundly, the charge is a failure to do good.

So what do we make of such a parable today? How can we find ourselves in the company of God's blessed? How can we meet Jesus? The parable doesn't mince words. You care for and serve people in need. You love them as though you were loving Christ . . . because you are. You don't love them because of the reward that follows. You don't minister to needs because that gives you a golden crown at the end. You don't serve others as a church growth strategy. That's not why the parable confers God's blessing on the first group. Blessing comes from love given unconditionally: without strings attached, without insuring that Christ really dwells inside that other person before extending a hand or taking out a wallet.

How do we practice such love? We begin by remembering how God loves us: graciously, persistently, even (or especially) when love and faith do not flow in return from those served. Only when we know ourselves so loved can we risk offering such love in return. Only then does our service and ministry mature into a freely rendered expression of thanksgiving for what God has already given us.

The parable implies that without such remembrance and practice our vision will be parochial. Our spiritual formation will be navel-gazing. Our stewardship will be fraud. Our evangelism will be institutional maintenance. We meet Jesus in the face of human need. What greater opportunity graces our lives than the possibility of encountering Christ? The sacrament of Communion feeds us at a table where Christ becomes present to us in mystery. But this parable suggests another "sacrament" of Christ's presence awaits us, even more mysterious.

I was hungry and you gave me food,
I was thirsty and you gave me something to drink,
I was a stranger and you welcomed me,
I was naked and you gave me clothing,
I was sick and you took care of me,
I was in prison and you visited me.

We need not wait to gather at table. We need not wait for the intonement of words of institution. When we break the bread of human compassion, when we share the cup of love poured out without condition, the parable ends and the life of sacramental service begins. For there we meet Jesus.

In whose eyes will I see yours today? May I tend to your children, O God, as though I am tending to you, for I am. In Jesus' name. Amen.

Spiritual Exercise

Look at the next person you see as if you are looking at Christ. Look at the needs that individual bears as if looking on a need borne by Christ. What will you do: not because you must but because you may?

Epilogue

FINAL DAYS OF HOLY WEEK

*W*e have journeyed through Lent accompanied by Jesus' parables. They have reminded us of the holy possibilities nestled in life's simple gifts. Parables of contrast have helped us see more clearly the distinctiveness of God's sovereign realm. Stories rooted in elements of nature have underscored the earthy nature of grace and our own embodiment of trust. Parables of relationships and responsibilities have drawn upon ordinary human interaction to illustrate extraordinary divine calls to live in faithfulness. We have seen in stories of customs and choices the need to recast our lives in solidarity with God's realm. In parables of upheaval and surprise we have seen how God's realm has the power to turn this world and our lives inside out and upside down for the sake of grace.

That journey toward Lent now comes to a head in the remembered events of Holy Week. Words that may have seemed veiled or oblique now come into sharp focus through meal and cross, tomb and rising. Once more parables will companion us. A wedding banquet offers foretaste of an upper room where Jesus shared bread and wine with followers and betrayers in anticipation of God's kingdom banquet. Wicked tenants will presage vigils kept before the violence of crosses. A grain of wheat will urge us toward quiet hope in those shades we know as death and despair. And finally, the story of Easter will serve as a parable waiting to be finished by our response to the incredible word of a risen Christ.

Holy Week awaits. Jesus still speaks in parables. May we listen for the words of God's realm in the (com)passion of Jesus the Christ.

Maundy Thursday: Gathered as Guests

The Wedding Banquet   *Matthew 22:1-14*

"Come, Lord Jesus, be our guest, and let this food to us be blessed." These words form the first table blessing I learned. My family sat at the evening meal with bowed heads and closed eyes and recited this simple rhyme inviting Jesus to be our guest.

"Be our guest." When you think about it, the words are presumptuous on our part. We say "be our guest" to the one who bids us come this night to an upper room where all is prepared for us. We utter "be our guest" to the one who invites comparison of bread broken at this night's table with his own body and the cup poured out with his own life's blood. We whisper as from afar "be our guest" to the one soon to be betrayed, denied, and deserted by those he gathered as guests. Maundy Thursday's table leads to a garden, then a trial and then a crucifixion. When Jesus hears us say, "Be our guest," might he not recall the treatment of the guest after Maundy Thursday's table? Is it worth the risk?

For guests and hosts alike, tables bring risk. Risk serves as a strong undercurrent in the parable Jesus tells of the wedding banquet in Matthew. Set aside for the moment the inclination to allegorize whom Jesus meant or whom Matthew's community heard in its characters. Look at the risks! A king determines to offer a wedding banquet for an heir, but what if no one comes? Servants carry out news of the invitation for table fellowship, only to be mistreated and killed by those invited. Those who had been bid to attend a wedding banquet instead set into motion their own funeral wakes. The king invites others from a seemingly far less elite group. One of them, who understandably shows up without proper dress, finds himself cast out into "outer darkness." What was he thinking, coming as a guest unprepared?

Then again: what are *we* thinking when we come as a guest to Maundy Thursday's table? What preparations have we made, and what may we have lost sight of?

Not too many years ago I sat at table with others for a Maundy Thursday observance. We observed the tradition of the seder meal, remembering how the church adopted that meal of deliverance from Egypt into a meal of cruciform deliverance. During one of the times in which the liturgy allowed for conversation as we ate, one small group bantered around the recent invasion of Iraq. Much bravado followed about the progress of the war and the certainty of Saddam's end. I remember thinking at that moment how totally out of place that conversation was, how incongruous with a Messiah who chose the way of the cross over the sword. But in reflection it seemed to me how utterly fitting that incongruity was to Maundy Thursday. At those tables we replayed what surely was part of the first table: disciples digressing in words that missed the point of Jesus' words, promises of allegiance and unassailable following made only hours before darkness saw flight and heard a cock crow. We sat at our tables, in our boasting and in our silence, acting out that meal of old in ways oblivious to us that night.

That is the risk taken by the one who hosts: to invite to this table, as he invited to that table long ago, those who are the guests of grace, even when we are not its practitioners or witnesses. The one detail of Jesus' parable that seems pivotal to this point is this: the second wave of servants sent out to bring guests "gathered all whom they found, both good and bad." In the Greek manuscript of Matthew's Gospel, the scandal of that action is even more pronounced because "bad" precedes "good" in the word order.

Maundy Thursday continues to fill its tables with bad and good alike. We come: those of us who still fall away when night comes, those of us who just do not get what that bread and cup offer to us and then ask of us. That is the risk Christ the host takes at this table. We gather as guests not gatekeepers. We feed here on grace not merit. Like disciples of old, that point sometimes escapes us. We prefer our tables be reserved for those who are like us; sometimes we go to great lengths to insure we are the ones who do the reserving. But notice that the servants sent out with the invitation do not separate the good from the bad. The servants do not say yes to one and no to another. All are gathered. If anyone sends someone packing into outer darkness, we do not issue the order. If anyone, it will be the one who makes room at the table for Judas, Peter, and all the others. It will be the one who seeks us with a love that will not let us go.

God in Christ takes the enormous risk of gathering us as guests. We have been graced by an invitation to the table this night. Let us keep the feast and stay faithful in the night that follows.

We come, Lord Jesus, to be your guests.

God in Christ, what love you show to make room for me and for all at your table. May I, in turn, be mindful of that love and be faithful in its practice. Amen.

SPIRITUAL EXERCISE

If possible attend a Maundy Thursday observance this night. Be aware of the gifts set at its table: bread, cup, and cross. Receive Christ's invitation as personal to you: to come, to eat, to find your place and your vocation in grace.

Good Friday: Who Holds the Future?

The Wicked Tenants   *Mark 12:1-12*

Some years ago *60 Minutes* interviewed a newly elected member of the British Parliament from Belfast, Northern Ireland. What made the election newsworthy was her open support of the Irish Republican Army, a group viewed by many at that time to be engaged in acts of violent resistance to Protestant (and British) control of Northern Ireland. Given the religious dimension of the violence in that troubled nation, the interviewer understandably pursued that line of questioning. Given the Parliament member's strong support of the IRA, the interviewer asked her: "Is God on your side?" Her reply was unnerving, both in its seriousness and implications: "God is on the side of the winner." At the risk of oversimplifying, she was declaring that the outcome of events reveals God's favor or "siding." For her, finding God is not a difficult search for right or wrong, moral or immoral but simply in identifying who is left on top of the heap when the smoke has cleared and the killing is over.

Such opportunism stamps this parable from Mark. The tenants perceive that life belongs to those willing and determined to succeed at any cost. An absentee landlord has allowed them the favorable chance to stake out their claims on land he has set them to work upon. The servants sent to collect his due are easily, and gradually more brutally, turned away empty. Possession of that vineyard and its produce has become the one end by which the tenants measure all actions. Even when the owner finally sends his son, the tenants seize an opportunity not to make peace but to make their strongest claim. They kill the son. The heir is gone. The land will be theirs. God must be on their side, for the future now belongs to them.

Momentarily.

As the parable ends, those left standing on top of the heap of history simply become another layer of sedimentary failures. The violence by which they lived becomes the curse by which they die. The vineyard passes on to other hands. Jesus elsewhere tells equally stern stories but not often. And now he strikes a raw nerve. The religious authorities of his day are infuriated, hearing in these words an indictment of their own poor stewardship of God's good purposes. Fear delays their intent to arrest—but not for long. In a few short days they have the teller of parables arrested in the middle of the night and crucified in the heat of the day.

And why not? God is on the side of the winner.

At approximately three o'clock on that Friday now called Good, who could argue the point? This threat to the future has been executed. Roman power efficiently dispatches a misguided rabbi and two thieves from the land of the living. The future belongs to those left standing at the end of the day. And at the end of this day Jesus stood no more. The one who told a story of a beloved son put to death out of envy became the story himself.

It is a story and a strategy repeated again and again among us. Brute force. Political opportunism. Kill or be killed. Only the strong survive. Do unto others before they do unto you. The name and context may change from generation to generation, but the core attitude remains the same. God is on the side of the winner. To the victor go the spoils.

We do well to linger in the shadows of Good Friday to appreciate the power and seduction of such logic. We do well to linger in the shadows of Good Friday to reflect on our own complicity in its continuing unfoldings among us. We may not be executioners who drive nails or plotters of another's demise. But we may at times yield to those seemingly smaller killings of spirit and hope that over time contribute to the stigmata of Christ's wounds by wounding others. We may at times be seduced by self-serving ends that justify any means. We may give in to the illusion that God is on the side of the last one standing in our view and time.

But the parable reminds us that views and times change. The tenants succeed only momentarily. By neglecting the truth of the vineyard's owner, they neglect the force of a future beyond their control and manipulation.

What does that perspective bring to our vigil of Good Friday? Religious authorities enforced their purpose. Rome executed Jesus. We are not yet at Easter morning, so we still grieve the shadow cast by an embodied crucifix. But conspirators and capital punishers have overlooked the force of a future beyond their control and manipulation. True, at the end of the day Jesus no longer stands. But in the chill of this day's closing, as from a still unseen distance, come whisperings. A story told of a vineyard's owner who will not be forever denied. A closing word of a stone rejected soon to become a cornerstone. A future that belongs not to the last one standing but to the one(s) God at the last "stands up": in Greek, *anastasis*; in English, *resurrects*.

Holy God, help me to trust so in your future that I may live faithfully today. Amen.

SPIRITUAL EXERCISE

Read one of the Crucifixion accounts in the Gospels. If possible, as you do so listen to a meditative piece of music such as Samuel Barber's *Adagio for Strings*. Where in that story and in this day do you experience hope that encourages you to live in trust of God's future, come what may?

Holy Saturday: Burial or Planting?

A Grain of Wheat   *John 12:23-24*

It was our second evening in Austria, after a day of cable cars into, then out of, the mountains and walking the streets of Innsbruck. We returned to a small Tyrolean restaurant where we had eaten the night before. The nonsmoking room, however, was filled this evening—as was the regular dining area. We started to walk back toward the door, when a waitress motioned us to a back room we had not seen. We had the room to ourselves. Almost. In perusing the room's knotty wood paneling and candled tables, we saw it hanging in a corner reaching to the ceiling—a carved wooden crucifix, not quite a meter tall. The sight in itself did not surprise us, for we had noticed crucifixes and crosses of various sizes all across the city and even atop the peaks we ascended by cable car. What made this particular crucifix distinctive was its adorning by four dried ears of corn, a string tying their husks around the feet of Jesus. On at least one of the ears, several rows of kernels at the bottom appeared to have already dropped off.

I have seen a picture of a crucifix in Bavaria with ears of corn at the foot of the cross. Dated in October, the corn perhaps was an expression of gratitude (or prayer for) good harvests. We saw the crucifix in the restaurant only a few days before Palm Sunday, so I cannot say whether dried ears of corn on a crucifix is an Austrian Easter custom. But as I write this less than ten days after seeing the crucifix, it provides a compelling visual for this day's parable.

"Unless a grain of wheat falls into the earth and dies, it remains just a single grain; but if it dies, it bears much fruit."

Holy Saturday is a day of stillness. Gone are the sounds of nails hammered and taunts slung and cross words spoken. Absent is the trembling of the earth and the tearing of the curtain and the measured request of Joseph for the lifeless body. All is deathly quiet, for a body has been buried in a vault of the earth.

Or is the more apt expression *planted*? That is the thrust of the parable: to transform the image of interment into seeding. The image does not readily come to our minds or hearts or grieved spirits. The image of planting and seeding is not our first reaction to watching the coffin of a loved one lowered into cement vaults. Joseph and Nicodemus did not look upon their task that day as sowers. The women who prepared spices on this day of quiet did not consider themselves to be preparing the body for a surprising return. No, they simply kept the traditions of their time surrounding death, as we do in ours. They readied the spices and themselves to complete Jesus' burial.

We observe Holy Saturday with the gift (or is it the drawback?) of hindsight not available to its first observers. We typically spend this time readying flowered crosses, displaying lilies, and buying the food for gatherings of church and family that will mark Easter. There is much to be done, and we cannot pretend as if Easter has never come for us as it had not yet come for them. But our parable provides insight into this day's vigil. Its implicit connection of grain falling to the earth with Jesus' death invites us to patience and trust in life that is not seen and cannot be rushed. The object of Holy Saturday is not to get to Easter morning as quickly as possible. Rather, it is to give us time and opportunity to reflect on what it means to await life in the face of death—indeed, what it means to live life in the face of death.

Beyond that, the parable offers another clue into what this quieted day invites and evokes in our lives and discipleship. The end of the parable is not just in a seed planted in the ground. The significance of the planting comes in the fruit that results. As Gail O'Day points out in her commentary on this passage in *The New Interpreter's Bible*, fruit in the Gospel of John serves as a metaphor for the community of faith. The creation of community serves as the purpose of the gift of this "planting," as Jesus makes clear in a subsequent verse. "And I, when I am lifted up from the earth, will draw all people to myself" (John 12:32).

The gift we await on Easter morning is not just what happens to me and what hope and destiny I have in Jesus Christ. The harvest of Easter morning comes in the community that God calls into being and that the Spirit empowers for mission. Such a harvest takes time and preparation. It takes individuals and communities willing to see their lives not as self-contained vessels but as seeds of grace and love, justice and compassion, planted by God in the renewal of all creation. We are sown in life; we are sown in death . . . but always we are sown in hope.

Holy Saturday is, for me, a crucifix with dried corn. Where its kernels fall into the ground, there comes not burial but planting. And the harvest of that planting will be God's realm, whose light will mark the turning of Holy Saturday into Easter Sunday.

O God, in the silence receive my grief. In the silence till my hope. In the silence prepare my service. Amen.

SPIRITUAL EXERCISE

Plant a seed and work the earth with your hands. Then practice patience and hope. Plant a seed with a word of forgiveness or an act of hospitality. Trust in God's good grace to bring life.

Easter Sunday: The Unfinished Parable

Mark's Resurrection Narrative   *Mark 16:1-8*

"You are looking for Jesus of Nazareth, who was crucified. He has been raised; he is not here." Blessed with the hindsight of two thousand years of Easters, the church does not always do justice to the incredible nature of the news just announced. Nor do we fully empathize with the flood of emotion such words must have unleashed upon its first hearers. Those three women had just borne the brunt of history's greatest reversal: "He has been raised; he is not here."

It is a message whose acceptance depended solely on faith. After all, there weren't too many other resurrections that morning to confirm the possibility that such things do happen. The women didn't see a videotape that captured the exact moment of Jesus' rising. The angel did not point to a single person who could truthfully claim to be an eyewitness to the act of resurrection, for there were none. In the shorter version of Mark's Easter account (verses 1-8), the women do not even have the benefit of seeing Jesus. "He is not here" is testimony to, not evidence of, Jesus' raising by God. Such testimony requires an enormous leap of faith.

A leap, interestingly enough, that Mark's telling of the Easter story does not have happen quite yet for these women—nor for anyone else. Instead, verse 8 ends with these words:

> So they went out and fled from the tomb,
> > for terror and amazement had seized them;
> > and they said nothing to anyone
> > for they were afraid.

Some of the oldest manuscripts of Mark's Gospel end there. In fact, this last sentence in Greek is not a sentence but an incomplete phrase: "They said nothing to anyone; they were afraid for . . ."

Afraid for—what? Were they afraid for being charged with telling idle tales if they spread the message, as Luke's account of Easter testifies? Were they afraid for their lack of faith in Jesus' earlier teaching of rising in three days? Were they afraid for daring to hope these words might be true? Easter generated fear long before it birthed faith. I suspect Easter has the same capacity today for us should we risk being startled by its astounding word spoken in a graveyard that had never seen a rising before: "he is not here."

There is a second point to Mark's abrupt midsentence ending of Easter. Namely, if the story ends with the women afraid to say anything to anyone, who does that leave to announce the Easter news? Is it the disciples? The last word Mark speaks to us about them comes from the garden of Gethsemane: "All of them deserted [Jesus] and fled." They are out of the picture. So then, is Easter's witness to be this young man who speaks to the women? Perhaps, but he doesn't budge from inside the tomb and not too many folks go prying around in cemeteries looking for words to live by. Will Jesus then be the harbinger of Easter? Maybe, except that the message given to the women states, "He is going ahead of you."

That pretty much runs the gamut of characters in Mark who'd be interested in telling the news. All who's left is the reader, the listener: you and me. And that is precisely the twist of Mark's open-ended and parable-like Easter narrative: *we* are the ones invited to take our place on this momentarily vacated stage. No one is left to share the word of resurrection but us. And where is it to be announced and shared? The young man tells the women that Jesus is going ahead to Galilee, where they and the disciples will see him. Galilee is a place where encounters with the risen Jesus do occur. But on another level, Galilee carries a deeper meaning as to where the risen Jesus may be seen.

Galilee, for most of the disciples and the women, is home. Galilee is the place where people reared families, exercised vocations, and played out the ordinary rhythm of life and death. The news of Easter is not sounded primarily for the sake of sanctuaries adorned with lilies, where you might expect to hear such proclamation. The news of Easter is taken back to all the usual and familiar places of our living, where death's defeat is not a given. The possibility of new life and rebirth needs echoing in settings where we spend the vast majority of our time and energy, where our fears can be very real. We are Easter people: not because of where we spend Easter morning but because of how we bring Easter to our other days.

"He is not here" does not simply describe the status of Jesus' tomb. "He is not here" vocalizes Easter's marching orders to a community that dares to believe—and to live—in the power and hope of resurrection. "He is not here" stands defiant in the face of all the places in our lives and in this world that go about in fear of dying and thus in fear of living.

Mark's Gospel leaves the door of Easter ajar for us. Like the parable of the loving father that ends with uncertainty over what the elder son will do, Mark leaves it to us to write Easter's conclusion in those places where we conduct our lives and dare to hope.

May God overcome our fears and free our faith—for Christ is risen indeed!

Holy Jesus, risen Christ, having shaken off the tomb and death: write your raising in the handwriting of my life. Grace me to live an Eastered life for the sake of the world you love. Amen.

SPIRITUAL EXERCISE

Offer a prayer of thanks for Easter's gift of new life and Easter's call to witness to the risen Christ who "goes ahead of you." Reflect on where and to whom Easter might lead you to witness in word and/or deed. Then, this day or this week, follow through on an Easter act of witness.

Leader's Guide

INTRODUCTION

*T*hese session outlines will aid groups who use *Parables and Passion* as a resource in the season of Lent. The study builds on six sessions through Lent, covering one chapter per week. It will be critical for participants to read the chapter to be covered (and do the accompanying spiritual exercises) in the week *prior* to the meeting. So in your planning, make sure participants have the books at least one week ahead of the first session, with instructions to do the reading and exercises for chapter 1. You might meet as a group the week prior to the first session to distribute the materials, walk through the structure of the book as well as do some initial community building, and give instructions about the readings and exercises to be done each week. Sessions have been planned on the basis of a forty-five minute gathering. Each session consists of PREPARING, OPENING, REFLECTING, EXPLORING, ENACTING, and CLOSING.

PREPARING includes suggestions for readying the room, gathering needed materials, and your own preparations as leader. OPENING suggests activities, including worship, that will introduce the theme. REFLECTING considers the readings and spiritual exercises of the past week. Do not gloss over or rush through this time. It may well present unexpected perspectives or thought-provoking considerations not anticipated in the session guide. EXPLORING delves more deeply into one aspect of the weekly theme. ENACTING invites some action on the part of the participants, individually and/or as a group, in response to the theme. CLOSING summarizes and reflects on the group experience, makes any assignments, and closes with a liturgical act.

Thank you for your leadership! May these parables and readings deepen the Lenten journey you and others will make in the days between Ash Wednesday and Easter Sunday.

Materials Needed for Most Sessions

- Bibles
- Newsprint, markers
- Glue sticks
- Paper, pencils, colored pencils, markers

FOR EACH SESSION:

Create a worship center using a table/bench, candle, and cloth. The gatherings are not just "head" experiences but "heart." Centering around a tangible worship center will help affirm that connection in the ways that worship calls us into holy presence and not simply holy knowledge.

SESSION 2:

Session 2 asks that the leader find and display several art images or photographs of high contrast.

Week One / Simple Gifts

Preparing

Preparing to Focus

This session focuses on the way God's grace and sovereign realm come revealed in the common and ordinary things of life. The session will encourage participants to consider fresh perceptions of the holy in our midst. It will also reflect on symbolism and imagery from contemporary daily life that might serve in our time as the simple elements of Jesus' parables did in his era.

Preparing Yourself

Read chapter 1 of *Parables and Passion*. Do the daily spiritual exercises. Think of ways in which you find hints of God in ordinary things and persons. Imagine what subjects or objects Jesus might use today to convey the meaning of God's realm. What might you and others discern, say, in the workings of a computer—or the ability of two individuals to carry on real-time conversations even though they live thousands of miles away from each other? How would you tell such a parable? What would it reveal about community, about the hidden interworkings of God's realm?

Review this session guide early in the week to allow adequate time for preparation of its activities. Pray for each participant you expect (and those who may come unexpectedly). Pray for God's Spirit to lead you in your service as group leader and for the group as a whole to be open to new ways of seeing and hearing the holy in the ordinary.

God, direct my preparations, and then my leading of this group. Open my eyes and spirit to you all around, including in those who will gather. Open us all to you in fresh ways. Amen.

Preparing the Space and Materials

* A variety of objects for the worship center a variety (some clearly religious ones: a cross, a church hymnal, perhaps one or more items usually found in your sanctuary; other objects found in a home or community: pencil, computer disk, leaf, rock)

OPENING

* Greet participants by name as they enter. When all have gathered, welcome persons to this series of group experiences based on *Parables and Passion*. Underscore the importance of keeping up with the daily readings and spiritual exercises.

* Light the candle on the worship center. Call attention to the collection of items you have placed on the worship center table. Brainstorm what items the participants understand as clearly "religious" in nature or meaning. Move those items to the side for the moment. Invite learners to gather around the worship center. Encourage them to handle as well as look at the items not identified as religious. Have each one of them choose one of those items (more than one person can choose the same item). Allow time for participants to consider silently how that object reveals something of God (or faith or God's realm) in the way it looks, the way it feels, its origin, or its use. Have participants identify their object and in a couple of sentences speak of its revealing of God.

* At the conclusion of this sharing affirm the potential of all these objects not initially identified as "religious" to reveal something of the holy in our midst. Invite the group to think of Lent in the same way in these or similar words.

Journey is a common and ordinary experience: we travel from home to work or school or church and back. Jesus journeyed to Jerusalem. Yet on that journey, not just at its end, the revealing of God occurred in any number of experiences and personal encounters that on the surface may have been considered routine or ordinary. Our journeying with and toward God is not a continuous series of spiritual highs where God's presence and purposes are overwhelmingly clear. More often holy encounter comes in the routine of life, in the ordinary persons and experiences surrounding us. The parables invite us to see and experience God's presence and realm just beneath the surface in the routine and commonplace. Lent bids us undertake a journey that practices such sight and insight, where the exercise of our senses comes with sensitivity to encounter with God.

* Invite participants to offer in unison the prayer that closes the "Prologue" reading for Ash Wednesday.

Reflecting

* Ask participants to reflect on the daily readings and exercises from chapter 1.

  —What spoke most deeply to you in terms of affirmations, questions, or disagreements?

  With a large group of over twelve persons, form small groups to allow individuals more time to speak. After everyone has spoken, invite the group to identify patterns or themes that have emerged. If you formed small groups, preface this with a report from each group that summarizes the sharing.

* Discuss ways in which these parables and readings on "Simple Gifts" connect with the season of Lent. Those connections could include general comments about this season, insights specific to programs or observances of your congregation, personal disciplines of this season undertaken or considered by individuals, and events in your community and the world.

EXPLORING

* Affirm how Jesus' parables in general and those explored in this week's readings drew from common experiences, persons, and relationships to speak of God's realm in our midst. Notice that some of the images in those parables (shepherds, masters, and slaves) are somewhat foreign to modern experience. Identify everyday experiences, technologies, or objects in our time that would not have been part of the landscape in Jesus' day.

* Have the group select three or four images or experiences most familiar to folks in this day and in particular in your community. Allow members to choose which of those they would like to work on by writing a modern-day parable concerning God's presence or realm. Individuals may work alone or in a group to craft the parable (each person works on only one parable).

* When individuals and/or groups have completed the writing, read the parables aloud. (Allow a maximum of ten minutes.) Do the first reading without comments or discussion: simply listen to the story. Afterward discuss the stories and their meanings. Consider the images and/or experiences the church uses to communicate its faith story to the wider community and culture. How might such retellings as you have done here influence how your congregation goes about Christian education or evangelism or worship? In what ways might you bring this conversation, and these stories created here, to the wider church? Where and how might the traditional stories of Lent be retold in new ways and with contemporary images?

ENACTING

* Think about objects that an outsider would consider a common part of life in your community: a plant or crop that is seen everywhere, an ethnic "flavor" of your region, a style of neighborhood relationships. In what ways does that gift reveal something

of God's goodness or grace for life where you live. Identify which of those simple gifts of life in your community is most at risk. What are the reasons for that risk? What would be lost if that gift disappeared? Develop a plan, actions to take this week and also over a longer period of time, to ease that risk. Think of tasks individuals can undertake and some group action the participants would be willing to commit to. Covenant with one another for each participant to do at least one thing, individually or with others, to preserve that God-given gift.

Closing

* Summarize this session's emphasis through these parables on encountering God and finding the realm of God revealed in the most common and ordinary of experiences. Emphasize the commitment to carry through on the Enacting response. Encourage individuals to use this season of Lent as a time of heightening sensitivity to the ways in which God continues to use the common and ordinary in our lives. Refocus attention on the items on the worship center. Some things possess clear and obvious connections to our faith. But when we look deeply at creation and at other human beings, it is possible to encounter God or discern something of God's realm in any and every work of God's creation.

* Close with a sentence prayer, inviting volunteers to offer brief prayers. If possible conclude by singing "Open My Eyes, That I May See."

* Remind everyone to read chapter 2, one reading each day, and to do the related spiritual exercises. Announce the next meeting (time, place, and any assignments or preparation).

Week Two / Studies in Contrast

Preparing

Preparing to Focus

This session explores contrasts made in the parables and those we discern in our own life experiences between God's realm and things as they are. It will encourage and challenge participants to hear the gospel's call to new ways of faithful thinking and acting exposed by those contrasts.

Preparing Yourself

Read chapter 2 of *Parables and Passion*. Do each of the daily spiritual exercises. Consider how the qualities and hopes of God's realm stand in stark contrast if not outright opposition to business as usual: in personal relationships, in church affairs, in community and political priorities. Recall the images and examples used in this week's parables. What might you and participants in this session choose as an image from contemporary life to illustrate the disjuncture between what passes for life now and what God's realm promises and evokes?

Review this session guide early in the week to allow adequate time for preparation of its activities. Pray for each participant. Seek the leading of God's Spirit in your preparations and in the preparations through reading and reflection being done by the participants. Pray for a willingness to see and acknowledge the gaps in our practices of discipleship.

God of light, be light to me in these preparations. Pour out light as I consider what we may do and what we can do. Pour out light, not so that I can see everything possible, for I cannot. Pour out light, so that I may keep my sight on you—and so help others to do the same. Amen.

Preparing the Space and Materials

*   Several art images or pictures from magazines that show strong contrasts (such as a painting that has bright light and dark shadows or bright colors and duller ones) as well as contrasts between them (for example, an image with no people, an image of a single individual, an image of a large crowd). Display them together, either on or alongside the worship center or on one wall of your meeting area.

OPENING

*   Greet participants by name as they enter. As they gather, invite them to study in silence the images you have brought.

*   Gather at the worship center and light the candle. Ask participants for general impressions or reactions to the pictures and images displayed. What do they remember most from them? Talk about how the pictures, individually and together, rely on contrasts (in color, in light, in subject), and how those contrasts served to catch our attention or shape our response.

*   Talk about Lent as a season of contrasts. Invite participants to name the kinds of contrasts Lent summons in our thoughts and experiences. For example: a story about life that is headed toward death, an affirmation of Jesus' power in the narrative of his vulnerability (he can be killed).

    Recall how the parables read this week—like the images and pictures viewed earlier, like the season of Lent itself— employ strong contrasts to assert the nature and qualities of God's coming realm. Affirm that this session intends to help us explore those contrasts and others we may be aware of in our own experience for the sake of our calling as disciples. Offer this prayer.

Holy God, we live in the time between your realm's revealing and its fulfillment. May we boldly name where new birth and hard work could bridge the gaps. May we speak the truth of your realm's call and live that truth as Christ's disciples. Amen.

REFLECTING

* Ask participants to reflect on the daily readings and exercises from chapter 2.

   —Have individuals share with the group what spoke most deeply to them in terms of affirmations, questions, or disagreements. With a large group of over twelve persons, form small groups to allow individuals more time to speak.

   —After everyone has spoken, invite the group to identify patterns or themes that have emerged. If you formed small groups earlier, preface this with a report from each group that summarizes its sharing.

* Discuss ways in which these parables and readings on "Studies in Contrasts" connect with the season of Lent. Those connections could include general comments about this Lent, insights specific to programs or observances of your congregation, personal disciplines of this season undertaken or considered by individuals, and events in your community and the world.

EXPLORING

* Brainstorm words that participants associate with the quality of life in God's realm (such as *justice, reunion*). Record the words on a sheet of newsprint. Briefly describe what those words would "look like" if they were fully experienced now.

* Tell participants to put a check mark beside the two most important qualities of God's promised realm to them. Identify the two qualities that have garnered the most checks, and write each of those words at the top of two sheets of newsprint (one per word).

* Identify present experiences or situations in your wider community, society as a whole—or in your church—that serve to contradict or oppose that hope. Write those contrasts to that quality of God's realm on the appropriate newsprint sheet. Discuss how those contrasts counter or compromise the ability of others to experience that promise of God's coming realm.

ENACTING

* Form two groups, one for each newsprint sheet about contrasts with God's realm. Affirm that God's coming realm is not just out there in the future but a part of our calling in faith today (Luke 17:21: "The kingdom of God is among you.") Have each group consider how your congregation can live toward the promise and hope of that quality of God's realm. Deal with the reality of the contrasts listed, and in response to them develop specific and practical steps that can begin to bridge the gap between those experiences and God's realm among us.

* Assure groups this is not a "how to solve all the world's problems" exercise. This is a "what can we do, here and now, that will bring that quality and promise of life into our living now."

* Gather groups together and have members briefly share what they have come up with. Decide how to proceed from here, whether as individuals or as a group, and how to bring this to your congregation and perhaps others in the wider community.

CLOSING

* Gather the group at the worship center. Look again at the artwork used at the beginning in light of this last activity. Offer these or similar words of summary: **Contrasts bring images into sharper focus. Experiences where we feel the gap between life as it is and life as God has promised it can sharpen our awareness that faith moves us to fresh witness**

and new action. We are called to live toward God's realm, and that calling may sometimes cause to us speak words and engage in actions that contrast with values and norms of the wider culture. Lent as a season bears a similar witness. The path of discipleship and the road to Jerusalem stand in contrast to competing gospels of "name it and claim it" and "me and mine first." And the closer we move toward Holy Week the stronger and clearer the contrasts become in the life of Jesus—and in our following of Jesus.

* Close by offering a litany form of the Lord's Prayer. Explain that between the petitions of the prayer that you will offer, the group will respond with: "May your dominion come among us even now, O God." Pray as follows:

Our Father (Creator) in heaven, hallowed be your name.
May your dominion come among us even now, O God.
Your kingdom come, your will be done, on earth as it is in heaven.
May your dominion come among us even now, O God.
Give us this day our daily bread.
May your dominion come among us even now, O God.
Forgive us our sins, as we forgive those who sin against us.
May your dominion come among us even now, O God.
Lead us not into temptation, but deliver us from evil.
May your dominion come among us even now, O God.
For yours is the kingdom, and the power and the glory, forever and forever.
May your dominion come among us even now, O God.

* Remind everyone to read chapter 3, one reading each day, and to do the related spiritual exercises. Make announcements about the next meeting (time, place, any special assignment or preparation).

Week Three / Attending to Creation

Preparing

Preparing to Focus

The session will invite our attentiveness to creation in order to discern the movement and meaning of God's realm, following the lead of Jesus' parables drawn from the created order. It will do so, understanding nature as God's creation of which we are stewards called to exercise care—not owners free to do as we please.

Preparing Yourself

Read chapter 3 of *Parables and Passion*. Do each of the daily spiritual exercises. Sit outside or take a short walk. Notice the gifts of creation, obvious and subtle, that surround you. What might you learn of God from this place in which you stand or walk and from the parts of creation you encounter there? What can you learn of grace, of persistence, of discipline?

Review this session guide early in the week to allow adequate time for preparation of its activities. Pray for each participant. Seek the leading of God's Spirit in your preparations. As you do, call to mind how others in the group might approach these parables of creation. Is someone among them losing their sight or hearing? Do one or more others spend hours working the soil or caring for animals? What might such experiences reveal to the rest of your group about the way we encounter God through creation?

You have fashioned me with body and mind, with feet planted on this earth and spirit drawn toward you. Guide me in preparing for this session, that I may help others—and myself—affirm those connections of creation and Creator. In Jesus Christ. Amen.

Preparing the Space and Materials

* Elements and gifts of creation native to your area: flowers, stones, plants, crops, placed on the worship center and around the meeting space

* Hymnals and songbooks of your church

OPENING

* Greet participants as they enter.

* Gather at the worship center. Light the candle. Pass around (or move to) the elements and gifts of creation native to your area. Encourage participants to use their senses of sight and smell and touch with the objects. Ask individuals to identify one of the items they feel especially drawn to. Suggest that they silently reflect on how that item reveals something about creation as a whole and note any connection with their faith story or experience.

* Lead the group in a litany of creation. Explain that each individual will be given an opportunity to identify the object chosen and some thoughts on what it reveals of creation and her or his faith story. Explain that you will begin by reading Psalm 104:24 and that you will then read it after each individual shares. The verse is this: "O Lord, how manifold are your works! In wisdom you have made them all." Carry out the litany.

* Talk about how Lent is sometimes only experienced as a season of looking inward. The parables read this week and this session moves us in the other direction. For in looking outward, at the world around us and through individual elements of it, we may see something of God's purposes and realm. Offer the following prayer:

Open us, O God, to your presence all around us. In this world you have fashioned, in these lives you have created and called— speak to us. Transform us. Renew us in your image. Amen.

REFLECTING

* Ask participants to reflect on the daily readings and exercises from chapter 3.

—Have individuals share with the group what spoke most deeply to them in terms of affirmations, questions, or disagreements. With a large group of over twelve persons, form small groups to allow participants more time to speak.

—After everyone has spoken, invite the group to identify patterns or themes that have emerged. If you formed small groups earlier, preface this with a report from each group that summarizes the sharing that took place.

* Discuss ways in which these parables and readings on "Attending to Creation" connect with the season of Lent. Those connections could include general comments about this season, insights specific to programs or observances of your congregation, personal disciplines of this season undertaken or considered, and events in your community and the world.

EXPLORING

* Distribute the hymnals and songbooks used in your congregation. If they have an index, find songs and hymns categorized under "Creation" or "God as Creator." If there is no index, go through and find those songs as you are able. Post a large sheet of butcher paper or several pieces of newsprint. Have participants draw the images of creation used in those hymns, and/or how those gifts of creation in the songs are used to reveal something of God or God's realm. Assure folks professional artistry is not the point.

* Do a quick hymn sing of the songs, perhaps limiting it to one verse from each hymn. If the tune is unfamiliar, read the verse in unison.

* On another sheet of newsprint identify the gifts of creation you experience in this place (your town/city or the surrounding area). Ask: What would a stranger to this area remember most about the sights, sounds, smells, tastes, and textures of this place?

* Choose three or four gifts of creation in your area and assign a group to each one. Talk about how that gift could be used in a parable (for example: the kingdom of God is like—then the name of the object or gift, and then have participants finish the sentence or tell a brief story).

    Gather the groups together, and have each one share its parable. Discuss how these parables might help others in your congregation or community to see God or God's realm in a new way—and to value these gifts of creation even more.

ENACTING

* Select one of the gifts identified in the previous exercise that is at some risk in your area. Discuss what threatens that gift at the present time. Think of how the loss or degradation of that element of creation would affect this place in which you live. Think of what the loss or degradation of that element of creation would do to the heart of God, whose hands fashioned it.

* Identify ways that individuals and your group as a whole can respond to protect or enhance that gift of creation. Be practical. Be specific. Be creative. Covenant together to take action together and to do so out of a sense of responsible stewardship for God's good creation.

CLOSING

* Gather at the worship center. Affirm how this week's parables all used the gifts of creation to reveal the promise and hope of God for us and all creation. Review the actions you covenanted to do. God's realm begins here and now in this created order. Remind participants that as we act as faithful stewards of the gifts God has fashioned, we serve the God whose presence and purposes come revealed through creation.

* You may have already used it in the EXPLORING section, but close by singing "For the Beauty of the Earth." Invite the group to sing it not only as a song of praise but as a hymn that commissions us to be stewards of earth's beauties and possibilities.

* Remind everyone to read chapter 4, one reading each day, and to do the related spiritual exercises. Make announcements about the next meeting (time, place, any special assignment or preparation).

Week Four / Relationships and Responsibilities

Preparing

Preparing to Focus

This session focuses on how human relationships provide windows for discovering God's realm and purposes for life. It will encourage participants to consider our interactions with others, not only in light of the parables encountered in this chapter but as the everyday locale where we exercise our faith.

Preparing Yourself

Read chapter 4 of *Parables and Passion*. Do the daily spiritual exercises. Be mindful of the variety of relationships you currently have (if you have time, do the relationship chart from the Exploring exercise). Jesus' parables used a variety of relationships to depict the nature of life lived in the awareness of God's presence and realm. What do your relationships reveal about grace and forgiveness, about the responsibilities of living in covenant with God and others?

Review this session guide early in the week to allow adequate time for preparation of its activities. Pray for each participant. Seek the leading of God's Spirit in your preparations. Keep in mind the multitude of relationships and responsibilities represented in the group that will gather in this session. Be sensitive to those who may be struggling in a relationship and who may have a difficult time discerning anything of God's realm in that struggle.

> *Open me, O God, to the relationships you have set me within. Open me to your purposes in the time and interactions of this session. Lead me and lead us all to discern the ways of your realm that you call us to embody in our relationships with and responsibilities for one another. Amen.*

Preparing the Space and Materials

* Ball of yarn (keep it out of view until you bring it out to use in the OPENING activity)

OPENING

* Greet participants as they enter.

* Gather in chairs placed in a circle by the worship center. Light the candle. Call attention to the fact that in every other session objects or images related to the session's theme have been on the worship center or displayed in the meeting area. Today it seems as though there are none. But there are. They are beside us and in front and around us. (*Bring out ball of yarn.*) Relationships are the theme of this session, and this room is filled with relationships. Explain you will toss the ball of yarn (while holding on to one end) to another. As you do, you will name something about your relationship with him or her (served on council with her, helped paint the church last year with him, children in the same Sunday school class, and so on). That person will then do the same, tossing the yarn (while holding on) to another, naming something about their relationship. Continue until everyone has been "connected" to others in the circle at least two times.

* At the end say these or similar words: **Look now at our circle. Remember all the ways named that bind us in relationship. Imagine the size of this circle if everyone in the congregation was part of it. We live in the midst of a multitude of relationships. In this week's parables, Jesus spoke of God's realm and the life of faithfulness through the images of a variety of human relationships: some good, some not so good. But in every case, how we live in covenant with one another is revealing of and is in turn shaped by God's purposes for our lives.**

* Offer this or a similar prayer of invocation:

Move among us, O God. Move through our words with one another, move through our thoughts on relationship—that we may be prepared for you to move us in the lives we lead. Amen.

REFLECTING

* Ask participants to reflect on the daily readings and exercises from chapter 4.

  —Have individuals share with the group what spoke most deeply to them in terms of affirmations, questions, or disagreements. If you have a large group of over twelve persons, form small groups to allow individuals more time to speak.

  —After everyone has spoken, invite the group to identify patterns or themes that have emerged. If you formed small groups earlier, preface this with a report from each group that summarizes the sharing that took place.

* Discuss ways in which these parables and readings on "Relationships and Responsibilities" connect with the season of Lent. Those connections could include general comments about this season, insights specific to programs or observances of your congregation, personal disciplines of this season undertaken or considered by individuals, and events in your community and the world.

EXPLORING

* Have participants create a "relationship chart" following these directions. Write your name in the center of a sheet of paper. Next, write the names of those you are in relationship with, whether the nature of the relationship be family, work, friendship, or church. "Locate" those names on the paper in proximity to your name, depending on the closeness of that relationship.

  Draw a line from your name to every other name on the sheet. Draw lines in a different color to connect others on that sheet to those with whom they have a relationship. Look at the end result. In all likelihood you have something resembling a spiderweb.

* Continue to the next step: **Did you write "God" as one of the names? If not—good. Consider the whole sheet of paper as a symbol of the way God's presence and realm involves every relationship you have. Consider what each of those relationships has taught or challenged you about: the grace of God, the gift of forgiveness, the importance of preparing to meet responsibilities, or some other aspect of life lived in the awareness of God's presence and realm.**

* Form groups of three or four. Share and discuss with one another some of those insights into faith and discipleship gained from your relationships. Listen to what others have experienced; do not just declare your own and leave it at that. Invite the groups to recall how Jesus' parables in this chapter relied on less-than-perfect characters and relationships. Encourage those willing to share how such experiences from their own relationships served to deepen insight into the practice of discipleship.

* Gather the groups together. Affirm in these or similar words: "While we may not consider some of those relationships as involving faith or as windows revealing the qualities of God's realm, every one of them has that potential. In every one of them we may see and be seen in the possibility of God's purposes and call to live faithfully and responsibly."

ENACTING

* Ask individuals to work alone for this exercise. Go back to the relationship chart. Pick one that is of greatest importance to you. Pick another relationship that is in need of restoration. (Affirm that the same relationship may serve for both choices.)

Consider the connections between those relationships with others and your relationship with God. How might your faithfulness to God and exhibiting the qualities of God's realm deepen and transform those relationships? Be specific. Think of actions you can—and will—take in the coming week. They need not be large or dramatic. Especially for the relationship in need of restoration, first steps may need to be small. But resolve to take them. Relationships always involve the choices of others. But as much as it is up to you, choose to nurture and restore these relationships as you are able in some new way.

Closing

* Gather at the worship center. Remind the group of the last parable in this week's chapter: the story of the persistent widow, a story of God's persistence in relationship with us. Invite the participants to be persistent in the relationships they have resolved to work on this week. To be persistent in a way that is gracious. To be persistent in a way that allows, rather than demands, response. To be persistent in seeking the good for that other and for that relationship. To be persistent, trusting God's persistence will always be for our good and for our life and for our wholeness.

* Close with sentence prayers by participants, respecting those who do not choose to pray aloud. Offer this commissioning benediction adapted from Romans 12–13:
Live in harmony with one another;
So far as it depends on you, live peaceably with all;
Owe no one anything, except to love one another.

* Remind everyone to read chapter 5, one reading each day, and to do the related spiritual exercises. Make announcements about the next meeting (time, place, any special assignment or preparation).

Week Five / Customs and Choices

Preparing

Preparing to Focus

This session moves from parables drawn from customs of Jesus' day to revisit our own "customary" ways of ordering our lives, the church, and the world around us. It will challenge participants to examine choices made on the basis of such customs and the vision of God's realm revealed in the parables of Jesus.

Preparing Yourself

Read chapter 5 of *Parables and Passion*. Do each of the daily spiritual exercises. Make a list of customs that strongly influence the choices made in your church: customs about worship, about service, about organization. Make a list of the customs that strongly influence your personal decisions in family, community, and church. In what ways do those customs pass on valued wisdom? In what ways do those customs inhibit new ideas and risk?

Review this session guide early in the week to allow time for preparation of its activities. Pray for each participant and for your preparations of this session. Bring to consciousness in those prayers and preparation the customs—and choices—that currently impact the lives of those who will be a part of this group. Be open to the Spirit's leading in how to speak of customs that need to be revisited, and risks in need of consideration, for the sake of faith.

Guide me, O God, as I work toward this session. Help me to trust your Spirit close by, so that I need not be anxious about what will come to pass. May we draw on traditions that open us to you and, in so opening, allow us to see new ways and think new thoughts. In Jesus Christ. Amen.

Preparing the Space and Materials

* Newsprint, markers

OPENING

* Greet participants as they enter.

* Engage in the following exercise with partners. One asks the other: "(Name), why do you follow Jesus?" The other answers in a single sentence (*no* long explanations). The first responds, "Thank you" and then asks the question again: "(Name), why do you follow Jesus?" The second then replies with another (and different) single-sentence response. This back-and-forth process continues for three minutes. At that time, the partners switch roles and the one who asked gives the answers and the one who answered asks the question.

* At the end of this time, gather as a group at the worship center. Invite responses to the previous exercise: difficulties experienced, insights opened. Light the candle and read Luke 9:57-60. Say these or similar words: **Discipleship is always a matter of choices. The choices are not always between the good of following Jesus and the bad of another option. Rather, the choices most often involve weighing priorities. In this passage from Luke the choices had to weigh actions and customs that were viewed as good by the culture: traditions about grieving and leave-taking. In the parables read this week other customs of the day became vistas for viewing the priorities of discipleship in the light of God's presence and realm. Some of your answers in the opening exercises may have come from traditions passed on to you, some from experiences of your own, and others a mix of the two. This season of Lent invites us to view how and why we follow Jesus—and to do so in ways that not only bring life to traditions received but at times open those traditions to new ways of following Jesus.**

*   Offer this or a similar prayer of invocation:

God of days past, whose grace and love we know; God of days to come, whose ways still surprise us: guide us in our time together. Open us to your word and Spirit, open us to one another. Make us pliable to your transforming presence that our choices may be renewed in our following of Jesus, in whose name we pray. Amen.

Reflecting

*   Ask participants to reflect on the daily readings and exercises from chapter 5.

—Have individuals share with the group what spoke most deeply to them in terms of affirmations, questions, or disagreements. If you have a large group of over twelve persons, form small groups to allow individuals more time to speak.

—After everyone has spoken, invite the group to identify patterns or themes that have emerged. If you formed small groups earlier, preface this with a report from each group that summarizes the sharing that took place within them.

*   Discuss ways in which these parables and readings on "Customs and Choices" connect with the season of Lent. Those connections could include general comments about this season, insights specific to programs or observances of your congregation, personal disciplines of this season undertaken or considered by individuals, and events in your community and the world.

Exploring

*   Post three sheets of newsprint (have extras on hand if needed). Title one sheet: Church Customs and Traditions. Title the second sheet: Community Customs and Traditions. Title the third sheet: Family Customs and Traditions. Form three groups. Explain that each group will rotate from sheet to sheet (no more than two minutes at each one). The assignment: brainstorm and write down the customs/traditions that influence and shape life in that particular setting. (For example: Church—our monthly potlucks; Community—identity as a Finnish heritage community; Family—we always eat one meal together with the TV off). Carry out the group work. Use extra sheets of newsprint as needed for responses.

* Gather as a group. Spend time silently looking over the customs and traditions identified. Invite participants to compare and contrast what appears on the lists. Focus now on the Church sheet. Post two additional sheets of newsprint alongside it. On top of the first write: In what ways do those customs pass on valued wisdom? On top of the second write: In what ways do those customs inhibit new ideas and risk? Discuss those two questions for every custom or tradition listed. Keep notes on the additional newsprint sheets.

* Move the conversation to how the valued wisdom and inhibitions impact the choices, past and current, of your congregation as a whole and individuals who are part of it. Review or read the introductory "Customs and Choices" at the beginning of this chapter to help connect this conversation with the parables and readings of this week.

ENACTING

* Read aloud the last sentence in the chapter's introduction of "Customs and Choices." Ask, **Where and how might we help bring new life into one or more of those customs identified on the Church Custom sheet as inhibiting new life and risk?** Encourage participants to be specific in their responses. Focus on one custom that seems to draw the most interest (check out your sense of that with the group). Develop further some of those initial ideas about how to bring new life to it. You might do this in terms of one or more of the themes from this chapter's parables: counting the cost, foundations, hospitality, wisdom that recognizes the times of opportunity, and/or risk for the sake of the future. Pray for God's guidance.

* Choose how you will covenant together to speak and act for the sake of this custom's renewal.

CLOSING

* Gather at the worship center. Invite participants to reflect on their experiences in this session. Make a point of thanking each one who speaks. Recall where this session began: in the give and take of why we follow Jesus. Say these or similar words: **Discipleship goes to the core of the Lenten season. We recall the stories and parables of Jesus not just to look back at what was said and done then but to look around to see how we may respond as followers of Jesus today. Customs and traditions form an important part of that following, but we are not limited to what has been done before to discern what God calls us to do now.**

* Close by singing a song of following Jesus such as "Jesu, Jesu"; "O Master, Let Me Walk with Thee"; "We Are Marching in the Light of God"; or one of your choosing. If singing will not work for your group, read the verses of one of these songs in unison or as a litany.

* Remind everyone to read chapter 6, one reading each day, and to do the related spiritual exercises. Make announcements about the next meeting (time, place, any special assignment or preparation).

Week Six / Upside Down, Inside Out

Preparing

Preparing to Focus

This session focuses on the way God's grace and sovereign realm come revealed in ways and folks that are out of character with the world's usual ordering of things. It will challenge adults to consider how such reversals beckon transformation in our following of Jesus as individuals and communities of faith. The session will also close out this group experience in hopes of further involvement with others in study and action that grow out of reflecting on scripture.

Preparing Yourself

Read chapter 6 of *Parables and Passion*. Do the daily spiritual exercises. Think about experiences in your life that have taken you in completely different directions than expected. What generated the change? What made it possible for you to follow that new path? Consider how God may have been at work to bring transformation. Where might similar changes or "overturnings" be needed in your practice of discipleship or that of your church?

Review this session guide early in the week to allow time for preparation of its activities. Pray for each participant and for your preparations. In those preparations be mindful of how the participants may be faced with life (or faith) being currently turned inside out for them. It is not often a comfortable place to be. But it can be a place and time of new growth and fresh starts.

Gracious God, guide me in planning and leading this closing session. Let it open each of us to your surprising and unexpected ways. Help us close this group in such a way as to encourage new experiences to follow. In Jesus Christ. Amen.

Preparing the Space and Materials

* Individual candle for each participant

* Display on the worship center and/or around the meeting area images or headlines that depict upside-down events in the life of the community or world that have reversed expectations or previous status quos. Examples could be a picture of the "Dewey Defeats Truman" headline, the Berlin Wall coming down, an unlikely victor in a local election, a child leading an adult. Most effective would be such symbols or images from your local community or even congregation.

OPENING

* Greet participants as they enter.

* Invite participants to look over the images gathered, at first without explaining what they are. After folks have looked at them, invite responses of what participants see in common among them.

* Gather at the worship center. Light the candle. Affirm that the theme of these pictures, as with the theme of the parables and readings from this week, has to do with reversals. Talk a few moments about the reversals depicted in these pictures or images. Invite participants to name others they would add, experiences that have turned the world upside down from its normal perspective on things. Mention that turning the world upside down is not an easy or swift process—nor does it come without tension, particularly from those who like it "right side up" and as it was. This session's discussions and activities will seek to bring parables' invitation to such turning to bear on our lives as individuals and as a faith community. Affirm that this session will be the last in this study, so built into those considerations that grow out of the parables will be leave-taking from

this group experience—hopefully in preparation for the next. Offer this prayer.

Holy One, Surprising One, move among us in this time. Open us to you and to your realm among us, and now open us to these words and one another. In Jesus Christ. Amen.

REFLECTING

* Ask participants to reflect on the daily readings and exercises from chapter 6.

—Have individuals share with the group what spoke most deeply to them in terms of affirmations, questions, or disagreements. If you have a large group of over twelve persons, form small groups to allow individuals more time to speak.

—After everyone has spoken, invite the group to identify patterns or themes that have emerged. If you formed small groups earlier, preface this with a report from each group that summarizes the sharing that took place.

* Discuss ways in which these parables and readings on "Upside Down, Inside Out" connect with the season of Lent. Those connections could include: general comments about this season, insights specific to programs or observances of your congregation, personal disciplines of this season undertaken or considered by individuals, and events in your community and the world.

EXPLORING

* Lead adults in the following guided meditation ("..." indicates pauses for thought): **Close your eyes. Find a comfortable position. Take a deep breath and hold it. Clear your mind of distracting thoughts. Breathe out those distractions. Repeat** this two or three times. If you feel yourself being distracted in the meditation, repeat this again . . . Call to mind an event or development you read in the newspaper or saw on the news that most troubled you this last week. . . . What did it involve? . . . Why was it disturbing? . . . Hold that experience in the light of one or more of the parables encountered: about fences broken down, about God's prodigal grace, about meeting Jesus in caring for others. . . . What parable speaks most directly to that experience? . . . What light might it shed? . . . What reversal might it encourage, and how? . . . Take a deep breath, open your eyes, and breathe out.

* Share the experiences called to mind and thoughts about them. If you have a large group, you may need to do this in groups of three or four. Discuss with one another whether, and how, the parables' stories of reversal bring hope to those situations and your facing of them.

* If you broke into smaller groups, gather as a whole and briefly summarize the conversations in each.

* Ask: What does it mean for the church to be entrusted with these stories of reversal and God's "upside-down" realm?

ENACTING

* Identify one or two of the experiences called to mind during the meditation and discussed afterward about which participants have a consensus of concern. Whether it is local or international in nature and scope, discuss what a faithful witness to God's realm and these parables would be in this situation: in words, in actions.

* Develop a plan to make that witness. Keep in mind that this is your last session together as a group. Decide on ways the plan can unfold without the group's checking in on it. Keep at the

forefront of the chosen words and actions the witness of these parables to God's realm. Be mindful especially of the final parable read and its core: Christ is encountered in service within the world.

CLOSING

*   Gather at the worship center. Bring the plan for witness, in idea or on paper, to this closing worship experience. Invite participants to name what they have found most helpful, not just in this session but in the entire study. Thank them for their commitment. Encourage them to carry out the ENACTING commitments not only from this and previous sessions but some of those they may have developed in response to the spiritual exercise components of the individual readings.

*   Have someone distribute the individual candles to participants. During this time, say these or similar words: **This week's parables affirm important ways in which God's realm and its grace will transform all of life. But notice that this week's parables, like many studied before, turn on the actions and faithful risks of individuals. A Samaritan who breaks the rules and ministers to a Jew. A father who is prodigal in love. The last parable, the Great Judgment, gives us no names for those who fed and sheltered and visited others—and that is well and good. For it leaves open the possibility that our names may find their way into this parable in actions of ministry and serving. That is the gift of all parables: finding ourselves in them, finding ourselves addressed by them, finding ourselves gifted with the grace of God's realm that fills them. Each of you now has a candle. There has been a candle lit in each of our times together during these sessions. Now the parables end, and the light we have received becomes the light we are invited to bring to this world. I invite each of you now to light your candle on your way out. And then to keep**

it with you where you pray and study at home. Light it then, and remember this group. Light it then, and remember God's grace. Go now in God's peace. And let the people of God say: "Amen."
Amen.

About the Author

JOHN INDERMARK lives in Naselle, Washington, with his wife, Judy, an E-911 dispatcher. Ordained in the United Church of Christ, John served as a parish pastor for sixteen years before being led to a ministry of writing that is now his full-time vocation. This is his sixth book published by Upper Room Books. In addition, John writes Christian education curricula for *Seasons of the Spirit, The Present Word, New International Lectionary Annual,* and *Great Themes of the Bible.* He has had articles published in *The Clergy Journal and Exchange* (a publication of the United Church of Canada).

In their spare time, John and Judy enjoy walking the area's logging roads and trails, puttering in the garden, and exploring the city of Victoria and Vancouver Island.

Other Upper Room books by John Indermark

Genesis of Grace
Setting the Christmas Stage
Neglected Voices
Traveling the Prayer Paths of Jesus
Turn toward Promise

To order call: 800-972-0433